MW00680554

THE **A-Z** OF
VIDEO AND
AUDIO-VISUAL
JARGON

THE A-Z OF VIDEO AND AUDIO-VISUAL JARGON

SUZAN ST MAUR

Routledge & Kegan Paul
London and New York

First published in 1986 by
Routledge & Kegan Paul Ltd
11 New Fetter Lane, London EC4P 4EE

Published in the USA by
Routledge & Kegan Paul Inc.
in association with Methuen Inc.
29 West 35th Street, New York, NY 10001

Set in Linotron Times 10 on 12pt
by Input Typesetting Ltd, London
and printed in Great Britain
by Butler & Tanner Ltd
Frome and London

© Suzan St Maur 1986

No part of this book may be reproduced in
any form without permission from the publisher
except for the quotation of brief passages
in criticism

Library of Congress Cataloging in Publication Data

St Maur, Suzan.
The A to Z of video and audio-visual jargon.
Bibliography: p.
1. Television—Dictionaries. 2. Audio-visual
education—Dictionaries. I. Title.
TK6634.S7 1986   621.388'332'0321   86–13041

British Library CIP Data also available

ISBN 0–7102–0640–2

To *Mike Wilson*

. . . one of the first to hire me and
encourage me as a scriptwriter, and
one who knows this business better
than a great many of us put together.

CONTENTS

FOREWORD

In recent years the a-v communications business in the UK, embracing the use of film, videotape, slides, overhead projection and audio, has grown to be worth (at a conservative estimate) over £350m.

It is a business with applications that range from training or salesforce motivation to higher education and explaining exhibits in museums. But it is also a multi-disciplinary business, borrowing techniques, ideas (and jargon) from the worlds of film, television, photography and sound engineering. That may put some people off. But as industry, the economy and our social structure become even more complex – just one result of the information society's tendency to bombard us with detail – we must ourselves learn to communicate our ideas and/or decisions clearly and persuasively. Otherwise, we will not be heard.

In the business and educational worlds the use of a-v is not a gimmick or some kind of management toy for would-be Hollywood producers; it is a tool as serious and important as established disciplines such as accounting or market research.

The companies and organisations who have become professional and proficient in their use of the various a-v media have undoubtedly benefited from the process, simply by, in some instances, generating clarity about their communications objectives. This has enabled them to specify both an audience and the message that should be transmitted.

Others have not fared so well because they have not sought any understanding of the media involved, regarding them as magic *panacea* which will make all the problems go away. They might have been sold the media in that way – the modern equivalent of pills from chalk – but inefficient users and the great mass of companies and organisations which have only toyed with the idea of using the a-v media now have a great deal of learning to do.

Foreword

In that context this book, which seeks to expound the structure of the a-v business as well as guiding the reader through the inevitable jargon, has an important job to do.

Ten years ago the a-v industry was all about film, filmstrip and overhead projectors. Today it is still about those media, but it is also about videotape and video disks, multi-image shows and all the trappings of broadcast television and live theatre.

The technology has expanded to become more useful to a greater number of communicators, expanding the market in the process. Put simply, you can achieve results with videotape (as just one example) that would have been inconceivable using an overhead projector.

But in the process new problems – including the jargon – have emerged and, very gradually, come to be accepted as a kind of verbal shorthand. As Suzan St Maur says (on p. 10), 'with a young industry like this it is hard to specify which definition is accurate. . . guidelines are being developed as the business grows'.

That process of growth and definition continues, and this book cannot represent more than a snapshot of where the a-v business is *now* and what it is calling things now. However, it is a snapshot which will help anyone serious about the need to communicate to do so more effectively and more professionally.

Peter Lloyd
Editor, *Audio-Visual* magazine
25 June 1986

ACKNOWLEDGMENTS

First of all, I'd like to thank three good friends: Jonathon Green, for his excellent additional jargon input; Ashley Mote, for his valuable comments and advice; and Penny Wells, for her superbly high-tech word processing. Secondly, I'd like to thank all my clients and colleagues, without whose help and expertise I'd never have learned about this business in the first place. And finally, grateful thanks to Peter Lloyd for his time and helpful guidance.

Suzan St Maur

CHAPTER 1
VIDEO AND
AUDIO-VISUAL
PRODUCTIONS:
what they are, and what they do

Video and audio-visual work can be and often is taken to mean a wide variety of things. You'll hear the term used in the context of corporate videotape programmes, educational slide–tape programmes, conferences, industrial documentaries, training films and many more. These categories are all defined in the later pages of this book, so there seems little point in going into their finer details here. What *is* needed at the beginning of this book is a more general overview of the role video, AV and related disciplines play in our working lives.

Communications has become a 'buzz' word of our age. And everyone knows that, with the advent of modern electronics and other technologies, the budding audio-visual media of the first half of this century – film and 'magic lantern' slide projectors – have metamorphosed into the bewildering array of communications possibilities we can choose from now. The only common denominator amongst them all – synchronised sound and vision – can be cast in umpteen different roles, depending on what's needed and how much money is on the table.

The purpose of all these widely varying types of audio-visual communication, in the context of the business and educational world at least, is to communicate information in a way that is both easily absorbed and well retained. Any retailer of audio-visual hardware will tell you that the retention rate of a presentation which combines synchronised sound and pictures is more than twice that of a sound-only presentation. And this ratio

1

applies also to live speakers; what is said by a speaker will be retained more than twice as accurately if supported by interesting slides or by a videotape back-up as compared to a simple spoken presentation.

It is also said that audio-visual communications appear to have knocked the written word and printed picture into a cocked hat. Although this is something of a sweeping statement, in many instances it is true. In employee communications, for example, the tried and tested company newsletter is more likely to be used to catch drips from coffee cups than it is to be read cover to cover. In contrast, the in-company video magazine programme, with its similarity to broadcast television news, will evoke a sit-up-and-take-notice response – in true Pavlovian fashion – in all but the most hard-bitten viewer.

With most of our white-collar workers now either owning home videocassette recorders or wishing they did, nearly all concerned in business-to-business and educational communications are truly entrenched in the video age. No longer do smart organisations rest contented with corporate brochures; everyone must now make the film of the book. And, once again, the retention figures attainable from a corporate story told on videotape are higher than those based on readership of a brochure or document.

On the training/educational side, the days of the formal classroom are fast becoming outdated and outpriced. It's rapidly getting to the point where, in order that executives and staff remain cost-effective and companies remain profitable, the classroom must be brought to the work station. Senior staff and executives are too busy keeping the company going to take time off to train others. The answer? Inter-active video-disk training systems with one-to-one teaching that requires the minimum amount of upheaval and offers uniform standards of instruction, even when its two-hundredth hour of use is coming up and it's four o'clock in the morning.

Then there is the keeping-up-with-the-Jones principle keeping us all stimulated to move on to bigger and better things. For example, for a company or other organisation to compete effectively in its market-place it must be *seen* to be at the forefront, and if it so happens that the market leaders in that area are casting aside the old company brochure in favour of the company video programme or multi-image presentation, then new companies have to follow suit if they want to play in the same league.

Needless to say, the great move towards audio-visual and motion picture communications pays suitably high dividends, otherwise the business world would have reverted to the printed word long ago. Not only do these techniques benefit from high viewer retention in practical terms, but also from the more subliminal advantage of being associated with the sophisticated image of the movies, television and high tech in general.

A company which uses the latest – although not necessarily the most elaborate and expensive – audio-visual techniques will be seen by its competitors as a progressive, modern organisation. Just as important, it will be seen by its employees as a company with its eye confidently on the future – a particularly comforting and motivating thought these days. And the company will be seen by its customers as one which respects and values their custom enough to employ the latest and finest available sales aids – something which will inevitably influence their buying and impress on them the company's desirability.

So, whether the reasoning behind it is commercial, practical or promotional, the result is the same. Audio-visual communications are here to stay. As technology improves and expands, so will this business, and so will the number of people working within the industry, creating films, programmes, presentations and other software in order to communicate all forms of non-entertainment messages.

What we need to do at this juncture is to identify the main types of production – or at least those which exist at the time of writing – and see where they fit into the overall picture.

Videotape programmes

Let's start by looking at what videotape is. It is a system, not unlike audiotape, whereby both sound and moving images are recorded on to magnetic tape. It is played back via a monitor which is, to all intents and purposes, just like the television set you have in your home except that the tape is plugged straight into the monitor via suitable playback machinery.

There are several different forms of videotape, of varying quality and cost. Basically, the wider the tape, the better the

3

quality and the higher the cost to produce. Half-inch tapes like VHS and Betamax are the narrowest and offer the least in terms of quality. The sizes then increase in steps; ¾-inch and 1-inch, with 2-inch at the top of the league, being the best quality and costing an arm and a leg. Then you have the recently-developed very small formats; examples of these include Microvideo, Compact VHS, Video 8, etc., all of which use cassettes roughly the size of standard audio cassettes. However, these have limited uses in business and education, although their quality can be surprisingly good. A recent innovation of more significance from the point of view of business use is Betacam – ½-inch tape using light portable equipment and offering extremely high quality.

The likelihood is that there will be further developments along the same lines in the future – smaller videotape formats with quality as good as the larger formats used now. As most high-tech equipment seems to go down the miniaturised/transistorised/small-is-beautiful route, so does business videotape.

So, from a production point of view, just what are the benefits of videotape, and how do they stack up against those of other audio-visual media?

Perhaps the greatest advantage videotape has over film and slide–tape is that you shoot it and it's there; there's no photographic processing period to delay your seeing the finished product. When you're shooting videotape, you can watch what is being recorded as you record it and play it back instantly. Obviously, videotape – like film – has the advantage of motion and live action that slide–tape doesn't offer. It's also less expensive to shoot than film – normally – and takes rather less time to organise. Editing, although quite expensive, also takes less time.

Of course the real crunch comes when you consider special effects. With videotape, special effects can be created instantaneously, literally at the touch of a button or two. Even smaller videotape editing suites now have at least a few 'effects' on hand, giving the programme-maker a wide choice of how to jazz up a programme – often particularly welcome for otherwise less-than-inspiring subject matter. Special effects on film, on the other hand, are very much more complicated and time consuming. Virtually all special effects on film have to be done

4

through lengthy and laborious procedures in the film laboratory. Anyone who has watched documentary programmes
about the making of *Star Wars* and other sci-fi movies will recall
the incredible expense and elaborate processes involved in their
special effects. I'm not saying that *Star Wars* could have been
made in half an hour using videotape special effects, but, for
the purposes of this business, creating effects on film costs at
least twice as much and takes many times as long as would
twiddling the knobs in a VTR suite.

Now, how about the disadvantages? Well, there are quite a
few, and the number does tend to vary according to whether
the person questioned is a film or videotape enthusiast. A lot
does have to do with personal preference. However, we are
faced with a few inescapable facts, the most immediate of which
is the variation in television standards.

It is perhaps one of life's little ironies that, within the three
geographical areas where readers of this book are likely to
be showing programmes, i.e. the USA, the UK and most of
continental Europe, and France, there are three different television standards, all incompatible. The USA has its NTSC
standard with 525 lines; the UK has PAL with 625 lines, as
have all the EEC countries except France, which has SECAM
on 625 lines. Moreover, should you have the misfortune to
need to show programmes in some parts of South America,
they confuse the picture even further with their PAL M standard – yet another variant. What all these initials and acronyms
amount to is an unmitigated nuisance if you are attempting to
produce good videotape copies of a programme to be circulated
within these different areas. No matter how high-quality a
format you use for initiation, you will still lose something in
the standards conversion procedure which you must inevitably
go through before a copy of your programme can be watched
on ordinary videotape equipment by the viewer. And that's
not to mention the expense and inconvenience involved if a
programme is to be distributed internationally.

As this book goes to press the Japanese are working hard
on HDTV – high definition television – which will produce a
standard with 1,125 lines that's the same everywhere in the
world. But bearing in mind the enormous amounts of money
involved in HDTV, and the similarly enormous amounts of
money already wrapped up in NTSC, PAL and SECAM equip-

ment, it will be quite a while before we can look upon HDTV videotape as a universal standard for productions. One benefit, though, that HDTV will bring when it comes lies in the area of projection – currently another disadvantage with videotape.

Videotape seen through an ordinary TV monitor is one thing, be it 525 or 625 lines. But when that is blown up to full film-screen size, the quality diminishes and it becomes possible to see how the picture is made up of the lines (according to the real cynics, you can actually count the lines if you've nothing better to do). Naturally great advances have been made in the area of videotape projection in the last ten years, and it's true to say that video projectors of the mid-1980s give a lot better results than did the early versions. However these results can't touch the quality of 16 mm film, with 35 mm slides giving the best on-screen quality of all, perhaps with the exception of 70 mm film. Meanwhile videotape lies firmly at the bottom of the league table.

HDTV, however, with roughly double the number of lines currently used, should mean that video projection will eventually become infinitely more respectable. Until then, though, the use of videotape for projection purposes will be restricted, and film or 35 mm slides in multi-image format will remain firm favourites for conference and other large audience work.

Whether a programme is to be projected or not, we come to another problem with videotape – its playback equipment. If a programme is to be sent out to relatively remote parts of the world you not only have to contend with the TV standard used there, but also with the more basic question of whether or not video equipment is available at all. Of course, in less than favourable playback circumstances a videotape player and TV monitor are very much more idiot-proof than a twin-projector dissolve unit and magazines full of easily-spilled slides, but there is none the less the question of whether or not the viewers have the correct video cassette format (for example, they have U-matic, you've sent out VHS) and indeed whether or not the local hire company has any video cassette playback equipment at all which isn't going to chew up the tape and spit it out. Although it does take a little more time and dedication to thread up a projector and set up a screen, the basic truth is that 8 mm or 16 mm film projectors are around just about everywhere, and there are no format or standard variations to worry about. No piece of prose about 'video' these days would be complete without at least a mention of the video disk. This creation, which can be made either mechanically or with a laser and which looks and performs rather like an audio LP record, has two main advantages over videotape. The first is that the quality of sound and vision reproduction is usually very good. The second is that, unless you use the disks as frisbees or jump up and down on them, they take a very long time to wear out. Tape, on the other hand, does tend to stretch and deteriorate if you play it back a lot. Consequently, video disk is perfect for educational and training purposes – either linear or interactive – where a programme is going to be seen by a hundred different students in quick succession. The problem with disk is that it can only be used as a playback medium at the time of writing, although the boffins are working on that. So for now, it's useless for home video 'time shifting'; you can't record broadcast programmes on it, nor can it be used in the business or educational context as an initiation medium.

Films

If you have just read the previous section you will know that videotape creates a great many problems in the playback area and in terms of quality – particularly where a production is distributed internationally and standards conversions have had to be done. However, under normal circumstances, the further-most-flung factories, office blocks and educational establishments can usually lay their hands on a film projector, even if it is very old and wheezy. And it is similarly comforting to know that everywhere in the world the film formats and standards are identical.

It is interesting to note too that, even today, up to about 50 per cent of the material you watch on broadcast television anywhere in the world is produced on film rather than on videotape. Let us look, briefly, at why this might be – as although it is largely entertainment television in question here, it still does reflect on the work of the non-entertainment field.

Lighting is one area where film scores. Film uses a photographic technique, requiring less intensive lighting than video-

7

tape recording, so less artificial lighting needs to be used and more use can be made of available light. This can be especially useful on locations where there isn't a lot of time or space to set up a large number of powerful lights, and means that the whole process of setting up on location tends to take less time than it does with videotape.

Technology is catching up, however. The newer videotape formats and camera equipment are being designed around the requirements of speed and simple lighting, so it is reasonable to assume that perhaps by the mid-1990s the advantage of film which has just been outlined will have been overtaken by videotape equipment.

Of course, this leads us to an obvious question: Are the days of film numbered, and will videotape one day replace film altogether? There are some who think this will happen. However, there is one advantage that film has over videotape which even HDTV won't triumph over, and that's quality. Quality is the other main reason why a great deal of material for television, which could just as easily be shot on videotape, is in fact shot on film. There is no way that even the finest of broadcast tape can match the quality of 35 mm film, and it is even hard pushed to match the quality of the smaller 16 mm film on which most television material is shot.

Videotape, with the harsher lighting it requires and the rather flat, hard images it produces, simply cannot achieve the subtlety and finesse possible with well-lit and well-directed film. Of course these artistic criteria are not particularly crucial in the context of education or business documentary work where other considerations often have to take priority. Here, it is cost-effectiveness and efficient communication of a message which is usually at the top of the shopping list, and videotape is normally preferable for these reasons. However, with fictional, sometimes even abstract, productions visual imagery becomes very much more important – rather in the way that an impressionist water colour or oil painting may state the same visual messages as a photograph, but in a very much richer, fuller fashion. Whereas videotape is represented by the photograph in my rather laboured metaphor, film is represented by the water-colour or oil painting.

Additionally, over and above the fact that you can catch a great deal more subtlety of colour and proportion on film than you can on tape, what you don't catch through the lens while filming you can often produce in the film laboratory. You can accentuate the colour, focus and texture of the image rather in the same way that you can re-touch a still photograph. With videotape, although there are machines which can 'clean up' original tape, the possibilities are limited.

Whether to use film or videotape for a business or educational production depends on how much you want to spend, where you're going to shoot the production (location, studio or both), what you're going to play the end product back on, how many people are going to be watching the production at any one time (video monitor or large-screen projection), and so on. A major consideration is what type of equipment you have sitting in the cupboard; equipment hire is expensive, and the fact that you already have one type of equipment on tap can make quite a difference to your budget.

However, the simplest way in which to decide the often tricky question of whether to choose tape or film is usually to seek good professional advice from a competent production company, whose personnel are trained to assess each individual project and recommend the best methods for it. There are also some good books on the market, with which I wouldn't dream of competing here; they explain fully the whys and wherefores of such decision making, and offer very sound advice. Perhaps the best known book of this nature, in the UK at least, is *Video Production Techniques* from Kluwer Publishing. Somewhat inadequately named, this pair of regularly updated loose-leaf volumes gives a comprehensive guide not only to videotape production but to film and slide–tape too.

Slide–tape programmes

These are also referred to as 'AVs', which of course is quite wrong (although so is calling a videotape programme a 'video', and a large number of other such mistakes which you'll find mentioned in the latter pages of this book). Strictly speaking AV stands for audio-visual, which can in theory mean any form of linked sound and vision, but the expression has become such a way of life in this business that it can no longer be ignored and is therefore tolerated by the pedants!

There is one big difference between slide–tape and videotape or film and that, of course, is that there is no true live-action movement. However, this fact is not always as obvious as it sounds, particularly when you watch a large-format multi-image production using more projectors than there are days in a month and looking much like a special-effects spectacular in finest Hollywood Panavision.

We must begin, however, by drawing a distinction, albeit a faint one, between slide–tape and multi-image. Slide–tape programmes start very simply with one projector being told what to do by pulses on a simple audio compact cassette tape, which also contains a commentary and maybe a little music. This will either be projected on to a screen, with sound emanating from a separate speaker or two, or it will all happen within one viewing unit. There are a number of brands of these units, but they are all basically similar. They look rather like ungainly television sets, with a magazine of slides sitting on top and the audio-tape stuck in the side; pictures come up on a screen built into the device, and sound comes from a mono speaker located somewhere in the side or front. Programmes for these single-projector systems are normally quite inexpensive to produce.

From there we move on to twin-projector dissolve systems. The end result is very similar, except that you can dissolve from one slide to the next rather than simply changing the slides. Twin-projector systems are usually set up and projected over a distance on to a screen, but there are some very clever little systems which are all built into one unit and fold up into a bag not much bigger than a briefcase.

Once you get up to three projectors the portability and all-in-one aspects go out of the window – with one or two exceptions. A three-projector rig must normally be 'thrown' over a distance to a screen, either front- or back-projected. With three projectors, though, you begin to get many more possibilities of creating interesting visual effects, including simple rotation, slow flashing, good dissolves, and others, all of which goes a fairly long way down the road towards the visual impact of true multi-image.

With over three projectors you are talking multi-image. (Some people define multi-image as being images projected over more than one screen area, rather than basing it on the number of projectors; with a young business like this, it is hard to specify which definition is accurate, as guidelines are being developed as the business grows. However, for these purposes let us assume that multi-image refers to the number of *images*, not screens.)

This is where production techniques begin to get very much more complicated and expensive, although the resulting effects and quality can be quite superb. Multi-image is explained more fully on page 122; right now we will look at the uses of slide–tape and multi-image rather than at their detailed meanings.

Small-format programmes (single, twin and three projector) have the great advantage over film and videotape of easy editing and updating. To substitute a new slide or sequence of slides, provided that it doesn't involve re-encoding the programme, is a question of using one pair of hands and a couple of hours' work at the most; film and videotape require expensive editing time and a great deal of machinery. However nowadays this is really the only plus point small-format slide–tape has to offer the programme-maker, as even a simple production can cost as much as, say, a low-band (small VTR format) videotape programme.

Once again, there are a great many considerations to be looked at before you can judge which is the cheaper and more effective method. For example, a programme where there is a great deal of difficult location photography to be done – on a selection of oil rigs, perhaps – will be far cheaper shot on stills as a slide–tape show than on anything else. (The programme can always be transferred to videotape later.) This is because the cost of sending one stills photographer to swing from hundred-foot derricks in the North Sea, with nothing but a couple of 35 mm camera bodies and lenses around his or her neck, is a lot cheaper than sending a film or videotape crew with a helicopter-load of equipment. On the other hand, it may cost no more – and be considerably more effective – to have a videotape camera shoot around the interior of a factory than if you were to do it on stills, with the added advantage of permitting a live action interview or two in addition to the narration. The short answer, needless to say, is when in doubt seek expert advice. And think carefully about what you're going to play the programme back on; often this will be the deciding factor in choosing a medium.

One compromise which is popular at the time of writing is to initiate a programme on a slide–tape rig and then have the programme transferred to videotape for playback (as mentioned above). This way you have the benefits of easy, idiot-proof playback; setting up a screen, projectors, audio-tape and a few magazines of slides isn't that quick or easy. You will have the advantage of simple, cheap updating of the slides when necessary; and if you need to make your programme in several different languages, you'll find this method especially cost-effective. Once you've made your changes, or recorded your different language versions, you simply transfer to videotape at a relatively low cost. Transfers are done either by projecting the slides and videotaping what's on screen, or through an ingenious system of projectors and mirrors called a 'multiplexer'. The latter system, which can transfer slide–tape programmes made using several projectors, is fully described in the entry section of this book.

Multi-image is something of a waste of time and money for audiences of less than about twenty. Indeed the vast majority of multi-image programmes and modules (a programme stands alone, whereas a module is part of an overall presentation) are shown with the sole purpose of seriously impressing a point or two on the audience before them. And this is precisely what they do, provided they have been made properly.

A good multi-image module will knock spots off projected film or videotape, even if you have gone to the trouble of paying for 35 mm film. The quality is certainly better. Multi-image consists of *still* pictures, although you wouldn't believe it sometimes when a multitude of images are changing before your eyes; film consists of moving pictures, sliding past the gate in the projector with far less of a momentary pause than you get with slides. So because the eye perceives slides on screen for longer, the images appear sharper and more clearly defined.

Special effects can be spectacular with multi-image, too. Although they may not quite measure up to the stunning efforts created in movies like *Star Wars* or *The Empire Strikes Back*, multi-image effects manage to generate a lot of audience 'oohs' and 'aahs', and on a minute fraction of a sci-fi movie's budget. And when you're using a wide screen format you can achieve a panoramic look, with images moving from side to side in tandem with quadrophonic sound which seems to move physically with the pictures. The list of effects is endless, but these effects do require the expert touch of a specialist production company.

The whole point of multi-image is to produce special effects that generate rather more of an atmosphere than the two-dimensional aspect of the single-screen slide–tape production, videotape programme or film. That's why multi-image is often used as the *pièce de résistance* within a conference or other presentation, as a module, or as a highlight of a live speaker show. It is also very valuable for any communication to a large audience, where screen size has to be big; to show scale or detail; to provide impact; and within an exhibition environment, to attract attention.

Multi-image is not cheap to produce. The cost of slides can be high, especially when you consider that one five-minute module programmed on to thirty projectors or so can run up a bill for several hundred slides, all individually produced. However, the overall effect is suitably classy; you certainly get what you pay for.

Business theatre

Business theatre, as the term suggests, consists of a live presentation in front of an audience. Interwoven into that you may well get one or more of the types of production mentioned above, plus a few others. The term 'business theatre' originated in the United States, where it is even bigger business than it is in the UK. A business theatre event can be: a company's internal sales conference; the launch of a new product or service by a company to its own employees, to its dealers, to the trade press, or to selected members of the public; the presentation of the end-of-year results to a company's employees or shareholders; and so on. Smaller events, such as short presentations to groups of employees or customers, come under the same heading, although they won't necessarily be so elaborate.

Behind the obvious purpose of most business theatre events, i.e. the communication of information, an educational job if you like – there usually lies a more subtle but equally important proposal. This is normally of a motivational nature, and is sometimes expressed in an overall theme which runs through

13

the whole event. This can consist of such thoughts as higher sales, consolidation of existing business, cutting out waste, etc. And this is where the theatricality of the business can be used to the full. 'Themeing' of conferences and other live presentations can be carried from the main multi-image modules right down to the style of announcements coming over the public address system. For example, one very large conference in which I was involved had as its theme the phrase 'Taking Off with Company X'. The entire auditorium area (built on the venue's badminton courts) was structured like the interior of an aircraft; the stage area was designed to look like an airliner's cockpit, with back-projection screens built into the spaces where the giant 'cockpit' windows were. The sides of the auditorium contained a number of extremely powerful audio speakers and when the opening module began, while the multi-image pictures gave the impression of looking out of the front of a Boeing 747 on take-off, the speakers belted out a few thousand watts of jet engine noise. That in itself got a round of applause. Throughout the day all the speeches were themed appropriately. At intervals, a lady's voice announced tea, coffee, lunch, etc., to be served to 'passengers', and suitably costumed 'stewardesses' were on hand to collect and return 'passengers' boarding passes' (sent to them a week or so before the conference) at the door of the auditorium.

These expensive and grandiose themeing events can, of course, be brought down to a more modest size and used in the smallest of business meetings. And even in shows where no such themeing is required, there may still be a need for visual input in the form of speaker-support slides. These are slides which, although programmed in projectors, have no accompanying soundtrack and are pulsed on manually, either by the speaker, who will hit a button on the end of a remote-control lead, or by a technician who will follow the speaker's written script or cue light activated from the lectern. Although some speakers feel that slides to support their talks either are not worth doing well or are not worth doing at all, a presentation given with slick professionally-produced slides and a well-prepared and well-rehearsed script is infinitely preferable. Professionally-produced speaker presentations have been proved beyond a shadow of doubt:

14

- to reflect far better on the prestige and calibre of the speaker; and
- to get listened to and committed to memory with over double the effectiveness of any other form.

Which rather puts the dampers on overhead projector slides; they are now seen as (and look) rather amateurish when compared to sharp, bright 35 mm slides.

The mixture of media within business theatre can be quite complicated. The norm at the time of writing is at least half a dozen stills-projectors on to one screen, except in the case of small business meetings, where you might just have two or three projectors for speaker-support slides. The use of six projectors allows for a few interesting multi-image modules, with the speaker-support slides programmed on to three out of the six (you don't normally need more than that for speaker slides).

Assuming that your venue is large enough to accommodate audience, speakers, equipment and crew, you can then increase the choice. Videotape projection is popular, although the quality of projected videotape looks very poor when seen immediately after the crisp, clear colour of 35 mm slide. However, it offers a useful and uncomplicated way to show the audience a copy of a new television commercial or even to give the audience an almost-live message from an absent chairman or other senior person. Film projection can be incorporated in a similar way into the presentation. In some very elaborate shows, where there is more than one screen area, it is possible to project film at the same time as multi-image slides – all are integrated into one spectacular visual montage. The problem with these productions – known as multi-media shows – is that there tends to be so much going on on screen at one time that the audience gets a little bamboozled and doesn't really absorb a great deal of the message. Multi-media shows were extremely popular in the 1960s and 1970s, especially in the USA, but seem to have tailed off in the more economy-conscious 1980s.

Sound

If there is an odd subject out in this book, it is sound. This is because sound is used mostly as an integral part of the other four categories, although it can of course be regarded as a medium in its own right and has a limited number of uses as such. The main reason why it has been included as a category on its own, though, is because it has a jargon of its own.

Sound as part of videotape is very much an integral element. When videotape recording is taking place, the sound is recorded at the same time by the same machine, albeit on a different section of the tape – it gets recorded on to the master tape on its own little channel or section of the tape width. Sound as part of a film production, on the other hand, is recorded separately on an ordinary sound tape-recorder; the sound track is 'married' on to a later print of the film afterwards. It is because of this separate way of recording sound for film that you often see film crews using a 'clapperboard'; the director tells the crew to activate the camera and the sound recorder, whereupon someone snaps the clapperboard in front of the camera. The result is a marking point on both the film and the audio tape which tells the post-production people where the action starts on both; the 'clap' sound on the tape and the frame on the film where the clapper hits the lower part of the device represent an accurate starting point.

The sound section of slide–tape is particularly important because it contains not only the voice, music, sound effects and so on but also the electronic pulses or instructions for the slide projectors. Most slide–tape and multi-image sound tapes will have at least two tracks on them. Apart from the very small single- or twin-projector systems (which may have only mono sound), there are usually four tracks – one for electronic pulses and two for stereophonic sound, plus another for sound effects, etc.

Sound in business theatre can be a complicated operation, especially if you have to deal with sound from a number of different sources, e.g. a videotape projector, multi-image modules, two or three radio microphones, a couple of lectern microphones, an off-stage microphone, and the house system on which you play the background music while the audience walks in and out. The running of a system like this requires the expert hands of a good sound technician, both to deal with wires and cables that look like a large portion of grey spaghetti, and to work a sound control desk with sufficient delicacy to blend all the input sources without mistakes.

CHAPTER 2
Who does what, and why

Taking the whole of this business right across the board, production can be broken down into three main groups of responsibility. Productions are, in the main, made by any one or any combination of these three: the in-house production studio or department; the outside production company (and in the case of advertising commercials, the production department of a radio or television station); and the outside facilities company.

Before we go any further it is perhaps a good idea to define the difference between production and facilities, as even within the business itself this is often a grey area. Production consists of making an entire programme, film or business theatre presentation from start to finish. This involves everything from the initial concepts and treatments, through scripts and storyboards where applicable, right the way down the line to the finished product. Facilities organisations, whether they consist of one person and a dog or a cast of thousands, provide only a part of that process – and the part they provide is always a function that occurs *after* the treatment and script have been done. So, facilities can mean a company that produces computer graphics, that does cartoon work, that provides videotape or film editing, or that makes hundreds of copies of a film, videotape or slide–tape master. Many of these facilities outfits describe themselves as production companies, but unless they offer clients a concept service from scratch, i.e. they take a project from an initial brief through to completion, they do not offer true production services.

However, there is one exception to this principle. In the area of television and radio commercials, organisations advertising themselves as production companies seldom if ever get themselves involved in the writing of scripts and the drawing of storyboards. These latter functions are normally performed by an advertising agency or consultancy, although in the case of a client going directly to a production company (i.e. who chooses not to use an advertising agency or consultancy) the production company will normally find people to script and storyboard the client's commercial. However, although the jargon and terminology listed in this book apply just as much to the production of advertising commercials as they do to longer, more involved productions, the whole story of advertising is one which has been very thoroughly dealt with in other books and is not examined here.

So, we get back to the realms of the production department, the production company (or production service attached to a broadcast station, which functions in the same way as a production company), and the facilities house.

The in-company department or studio

More and more large organisations which have a regular and extensive need for audio-visual communications are setting up their own studios and production departments to handle varying levels of production involvement. This can mean anything from two people sitting either side of a desk, organising and coordinating the activities of a variety of outside production and facilities companies, to large departments with fully-equipped broadcast-standard video studios that produce regular in-company video magazine programmes as well as a range of video training programmes, of which some may be inter-active, plus one-off videotape programmes, slide–tape programmes and speaker-support material.

Obviously, a large international organisation which has truly recognised the advent of the video age will spend a great deal of money each year on audio-visual communications of many different kinds. Once the annual expenditure on such activities exceeds a certain level, the idea of starting an in-house department becomes increasingly attractive and economic. Some companies still prefer to retain their independence when buying in services, and will employ a small production team that acts as an overall coordination point for a variety of specialist production or facilities companies. Others who may have a more modest requirement, e.g. only for videotape, will contemplate the establishment of their own studio not only to produce

18

programmes but also to shoot them, edit them and even make copies to be distributed throughout their own network.

However, such organisations, no matter how well-developed their own set-up, may still buy in specialised facilities like computer graphics, special videotape effects and so on. They may also buy in the production services of scriptwriters, directors and producers. This is because, no matter how widespread the audio-visual activities of the company concerned, it is very seldom that it makes economic sense to install such specialised – and expensive – equipment or personnel. It is also rare to find an in-company studio or department that employs full camera crews or slide production staff; apart from very rare circumstances, this simply would not be cost-effective. And, whether it is co-incidental or not, you'll usually find that the highest-calibre experts in these fields prefer to work on a freelance basis anyway.

For a company to set up its own audio-visual production department and to justify the expense, there has to be quite a regular throughput of work. Some companies with a trickle rather than a flow of such work may merely tack on a small extra capacity to their advertising or public relations departments. However, the majority of companies that use audio-visual communications in a small-to-medium capacity, justifying only a token acknowledgment in terms of in-house staff, will engage the services of a production company.

The production company

Trying to define a production company is like answering the riddle 'How long is a piece of string?' Just as with the in-house production department, the production company can be anything from one person with a desk and a telephone, to a large audio-visual factory employing dozens of staff.

Where we are more likely to find a common denominator, though, is in what a production company does – creating total productions. The variation comes in on the subject of workers to carry out the different functions of such a process; the one-person-one-desk variety will hire in freelance individuals and facilities for everything, whereas the large organisation will provide all but a few functions under its own roof.

Not surprisingly, there are two very clear schools of thought

19

on this difference of approach. There are those who favour the small, tightly-knit production company which hires in freelance people to do all the key jobs such as scriptwriting, directing, camera operation, graphics, etc. The argument in favour of this approach is that the production company is free to hand-pick the best and most suitable people for the job, drawing on a far wider choice of personnel than would be the case with a virtual Hobson's choice of in-house staff.

One of the arguments against compiling such teams of free-lance people and small facilities set-ups is that these people get around, know what every production company and client is up to, and could present some sort of a security risk. And to be fair, there are clients who become nervous over the fact that some of the people working on their production may not be on the production company's payroll and may not therefore be sufficiently loyal. However, any successful freelance operator or small facilities outfit in this business will tell you that the most valuable talent anyone in their job can have is a tightly-buttoned lip. Anyone indulging in even the merest trifle of industrial espionage or disloyalty will only ever get the chance once; word of such undesirable activity spreads like the plague, with disastrous results for the perpetrator of the crime. And with competition among freelance individuals and operations increasing just as fast as it is for the larger companies, the last thing any of them is likely to do is jeopardise future work by leaking sensitive information.

Another, less serious argument against the small-is-beautiful production company arises out of the question of professional pride. A small production company's one or two directors may not like to admit to clients that they haven't exactly got a personnel register the length of Metro-Goldwyn-Meyer's. And it is true to say that some clients may feel more reassured by a production company with several employees on the payroll; but at the end of the day it is quality, not quantity, that prod-uces the best work. Most clients or organisations commissioning productions recognise the validity of this point only too well – especially if they find it out through experience of indifferent work having been produced by a large production company. It's what the production company does that counts, not how many people they employ to do it.

At the other end of the spectrum you have the large

production company that provides, under its own roof, almost every facility it's ever going to need. Such companies are found mainly in business theatre production, where, quite apart from economic arguments, there are very good reasons for having such facilities in-house. Speed, for example, is a prime reason. The speed at which some conferences are designed, written, prepared and despatched is often quite alarming; it frequently involves teams of people toiling around the clock in order to get all the work done on time. By cutting back on travelling, as well as avoiding the delays caused by the complications of work going on in several different places, precious time is saved.

Another benefit of the large production company lies in quality control. It is obvious that supervision is a great deal more efficient if all the work is being processed in one place, and many producers find it a lot easier to coordinate and control a production when they can physically lay hands on everybody concerned at the same time. And because business theatre production is particularly labour-intensive, quality control is as important as it is difficult to do.

Film, videotape and slide–tape production companies of a medium size – and it is in this category that you'll find the vast majority of production companies – tend to work to a compromise. Key personnel such as producers, visualisers, production managers, along with more junior staff such as slide-mounters and general maintenance technicians, will be employed on a full-time basis. More specialised, and therefore less frequently needed, people such as scriptwriters, directors, graphics artists, animators, camera operators, stills photographers and the like are usually freelance, although there are of course some exceptions. Medium-sized production companies will hire such people in on a time or total-fee basis, or will sometimes have some kind of retainer arrangement with their favourites in each category. That way the freelancer is free to work for other organisations and keep his or her earnings up, while the production company doesn't have to bear the strain of the high salaries these people require.

However, with key personnel of a more general nature on staff, there is a flow and continuity which is suitable for clients' requirements. Indeed many clients who are more experienced in the audio-visual area prefer the approach adopted by medium-sized production companies; they can have the best of both worlds, with continuity on the production/management side and the pick of the best in the country for specialised creative work.

Whether the production company hires in specialists and facilities or employs them all in-house, it must never lose sight of its primary job – to devise, create and produce productions on behalf of its clients. The production company's role within industry, institutions and education is to listen to the client's requirements, learn about the client's operation or business and then create the solution to the client's audio-visual problem with a production that meets as many of the criteria as is humanly possible. That may sound like an inhumanly impossible task, but there are many, many production companies achieving these goals every day of the week.

A word about specialisation

A large number of production companies will offer production in any of the main media, i.e. videotape, film, slide–tape, multi-image and business theatre. The chances are, though, that they will in fact specialise in only one area, such as conference work or videotape, but be able to offer any of the others by sub-contracting to other production companies or facilities outfits.

Some clients are a little afraid to put the work of one medium out to a production company whom they believe specialises in another. It is impossible to give clear advice in this area, because each case has to be assessed on its own merits. Some production companies, of course, specialise quite unashamedly in one medium only, and will simply turn away requests for work in other media. With the production companies that offer a total audio-visual service, however, the picture is not so clear. On the one hand, from a technical point of view, it is easy to see the merits of choosing horses for courses and having videotape productions made by videotape specialists, slide–tape programmes made by slide–tape specialists, etc. On the other hand, when a client company has established a very good rapport with a production company, when the production company's staff have come to know the client's business very well through, say, producing several conferences and business meetings for it – what then? If that same client suddenly finds

a need for a videotape programme, should he or she take
the project to another production company who specialises in
videotape but who doesn't know the client from Adam? Or
should the client go to the original business-theatre production
company, who may have to hire in a videotape expert or two
to handle the nuts and bolts of the job but who will understand
far better and quicker the real needs of the client's videotape
project? A question to ponder and one to which there are no
easy answers.

For the sake of argument, however, I will list the main areas
of production company specialisation.

1 Videotape – commercials, documentary, corporate,
  industrial.
2 Film – advertising commercials.
3 Films/Videotape – advertising commercials, rock music
  promotional productions, documentary, corporate,
  industrial.
4 Television – videotape or film, mostly for broadcast,
  although some will do non-broadcast productions.
5 Feature film – precisely this, although some will make
  documentaries.
6 Audio-visual – slide–tape, multi-image up to medium-
  format, and slide–tape programmes to be transferred to
  videotape. Some also make videotape programmes, but care
  must be exercised to avoid those production companies
  who don't understand the difference in creative approach
  and produce slide–tape programmes in moving form . . .
  boring and wasteful. Some can also produce small- to
  medium-sized conferences and business meetings.
7 Conference – business theatre, plus multi-image and film or
  videotape which are usually bought in or subcontracted.
  These specialists are experts in staging and theatrical work,
  and will act as impresarios, hiring in dancers,
  choreographers, set-builders, actors, presenters – in fact
  everything down to the performing seals. Because they are
  normally trained to think big, they are not always the best
  people to go to for small shows and productions, but there
  are exceptions, particularly if the client concerned is a
  regular and also uses them for bigger projects.

23

8 Sound or radio – produce radio commercials and other audio productions.

The facilities company

In general terms, 'facilities' here is taken to mean the machinery and relevant operators you need to make films and programmes. The most obvious areas are companies that hire out camera equipment and crews, and editing set-ups. Then comes the sound studio which, when sound is an integral part of a production (as it normally is), counts as a facility rather than as a stand-alone production element. After that comes the sound-stage or television studio which provides a suitable indoor area for filming or videotape recording, with plugs in all the right places, areas for cameras and lighting to manoeuvre in, seats and control panels for the production staff, people to make tea and coffee and fetch sandwiches, etc.

In most major centres of the industrialised world there are facilities companies that offer pretty well everything the film or VTR maker needs in one centre. Even huge organisations like the Burbank Studios in California and Pinewood Studios in the UK are, at the end of the day, facilities operations – albeit famous, glamorous and very large. For the purposes of this business, however, Burbank and Pinewood are perhaps a little too ambitious, and are so expensive that they would give the average production manager his or her first coronary. But smaller, more modest and very efficient centres do exist in most major cities and provide the programme maker with everything required.

Many production companies will buy in their facilities from different sources, just as they buy in their scriptwriters and directors. For example, they might use a superb sound engineer at one studio to mix a sound track for a film, edit the film at another address where there is an editor who specialises in that kind of subject matter, get their opticals (special graphics and effects) done by a further expert around the corner, and have the final dubbing and editing done by yet another expert supplier three streets away. Conversely, they may decide it's better to buy all the services just described above from one studio complex – and for a different project, that might well be preferable. In fact a lot can be learned about the quality of a production company by its choice of facilities suppliers and the ways in which it coordinates them.

Then there are the fringe facilities operations which don't really fall into the category of either facilities companies or production companies, but which have to be classified somehow. These are the people and groups of people who provide animation (cartoons), special effects like those you see in rock videos, puppet makers, model makers, location catering vehicles and personnel, animal trainers, casting agencies, voice-over agencies, stunt coordinators, etc. There really is no end to the number of such specialist companies and freelance individuals who work in this business. Many of them make their living (or would like to make their living) from feature films and broadcast television. However, in Europe at least, work in broadcast TV and feature films is limited, as indeed is work for those industries as a whole. In the United States the picture is rather more cheerful, but elsewhere it is largely thanks to the production of advertising commercials and, since the mid-1960s, video, AV and related work, that many of these people manage to earn a crust on a regular basis.

Some facilities companies, whose mainstream operation is, say, videotape editing and general post-production, may offer production itself as an add-on. In other words, although they specialise in a post-production facility for production companies to use, they can offer what the production company offers as well, should a client wish to employ them in that capacity.

Needless to say, there is some irritation caused in production companies by what they see as an attempt to pinch business from them. The real worriers among production company executives will avoid such facilities operations altogether for fear that their client will get inveigled away. Sadly, there's no simple answer to this problem and it is all too easy to understand both points of view. On the production company's side, you can see that the last thing they need in this already competitive business is the thought that they must compete with their own suppliers as well. On the facilities company's side, you can also see that if there is the possibility of increasing turnover through offering production, in an age when it gets progressively harder to keep turnover looking healthy, the temptation is hard to resist. However, let us not allow the problem to take on too dramatic an aspect. When truly professional production

25

companies work with truly professional facilities companies, for truly professional clients who respect them and don't try to play one off against the other in order to save a bit on the budget, the problem does not arise.

CHAPTER 3
A production portrait gallery

Although there are at least a hundred and one different types of production that could legitimately fall under the heading of video, AV and related types of work, it is possible to break them down into a few broad categories. In the pages that follow you'll see the categories outlined, with a description of an 'example' within each and how it would unfold in real life. However there are a couple of elements which are – or at least should be – common to all types of production.

The first element to establish in any form of production is the brief. This may be verbal, or preferably written, but whatever form it takes it must establish very clearly the background, the audience, the objectives and the content requirements. It should be produced by the person or group of people who are commissioning the production, then discussed and 'fleshed out' with whoever is to create the production. The quality of the brief is paramount to the success of the project, because no matter how good the production techniques used, a bad or inadequate brief will invariably lead to a poor result.

Another element which is common to all is the production schedule. This modest sheet or two of paper is often likened to the Bible or the Koran, and although deviation from its directions may not result in quite the same level of hellfire and damnation, adherence to its instructions is all-important. The production schedule is produced backwards, so to speak, with the first date to be considered being that on which the finished production must be available for distribution. The remaining deadlines are worked out from that. So whether you're producing a five-minute single-projector slide–tape programme or positively the last remake of *Ben Hur*, the production schedule is one of the most crucial jobs to be done.

Having sounded off about briefs and production schedules, it is fair to say that that's where the similarity between programmes often ends. And although this is definitely not a 'how to' book – there are plenty of good ones around already – you may appreciate a brief glimpse at well-ordered, written chronicles below, which represent what usually transpires to be controlled panic and manic good humour involved in typical productions.

The small videotape or film production

Perhaps the first thing that should be said here is that in general production terms – within the non-broadcast, non-entertainment field – there is very little difference between videotape and film at pre-production and production stages. The true differences occur in the technical aspects, of course, but primarily in post-production. Videotape editing and film editing use completely different techniques: videotape is edited electronically, by effectively re-recording the selected sections of tape in correct order on to a master tape; film is cut up, stuck together in correct order, and then re-processed in the laboratory into a final copy, so you can't see the joins.

The next step is to define the 'small' production – perhaps that term in itself is a bit of a misnomer. What would be somewhat more accurate is to call it a simple, inexpensive production, designed around an uncomplicated treatment of a straightforward message and shot on a low budget.

Let's assume that this typical simple production will include one or two live-action interviews – perhaps a top-and-tail approach, with a studio presenter (introducing and summarising the programme), and narration over live-action tape or footage forming the remainder. This would be quite a representative example of a low-budget corporate or training production.

- The in-house team or chosen production company is briefed by the originators of the programme or by the client.

Pre-production

- A scriptwriter is called in. He or she develops a treatment with the producer.
- A full costing is prepared on the basis of the treatment, and a production schedule is also drawn up.
- The treatment, costing and production schedule are shown

to the client. Any necessary alterations are made, and the client gives approval.

- A director is hired, if there isn't already one on staff. This may also happen at the very start rather than at this stage. In other circumstances the producer will also be the director, and sometimes the writer and director are one and the same. For a small production it is even possible for one person to do all three jobs; provided the production schedule is quite straightforward, he or she won't suffer too many sleepless nights. Anything other than a very simple programme or film, though, requires at least two, and preferably three, pairs of hands.
- All relevant locations, and a studio if the client or production company doesn't have one, are booked and confirmed.
- The script is written and a storyboard is prepared.
- The client is presented with the script and storyboard. Any necessary alterations are made and approval given.
- The camera crew is hired, if such people are not already on the production company's staff. All equipment required for shooting is made available – in this case, it's only likely to consist of a single camera, either video recorder or audio recorder (depending on whether you're shooting VTR or film), lights and power accessories. Some production companies which also have their own facilities will have all the necessary equipment; if not, it will have to be hired. In either case it will then have to be checked and any necessary maintenance carried out.
- Dates for location and studio shooting are confirmed, and all relevant performers taking part in the programme or film should be confirmed as available on those dates.
- If the production company does not have its own editing facilities, these should be booked at this stage of the production, if not earlier. Off-line videotape editing can often be done at the production company's premises by transferring the master tape on to VHS or U-matic and working it through on simple, inexpensive editing equipment. On-lining, though, must be done on as high-quality a format as possible, and although some production companies own this expensive gear, there aren't too many of them. Consequently it is likely that a good

29

videotape edit suite will have to be booked for the on-line at least. With film, a rough cut can often be produced on the production company's premises, although, unlike videotape, film editing – even the earliest stages – is best done by an expert editor on the highest quality equipment. Large production companies are likely to have their own editing arrangements or 'cutting rooms', but the smaller ones are likely to go to a specialist film-editing operation. There are normally several good film-editing facilities in major cities.

Production

- Live action shooting is carried out (both on location and in a studio).
- Graphics are prepared for inclusion at editing stage, and any other relevant material like library stills or footage is prepared.
- Rostrum filming/recording is done.

Post-production

- An off-line edit – or rough cut if it is a film – is prepared by the director, sometimes assisted by the writer. This will follow the approved script and storyboard.
- The narration script is re-adjusted if necessary, depending on the way in which the off-line or rough cut has been prepared. In some cases the narration script will only be written at this stage to form accurate links between freshly edited sections.
- The client is shown the off-line programme, or a rough cut of the film with the sound track played back in sync but on another system. This is sometimes called a 'double head', as both film and audio tape go through the same machine. Once any necessary changes have been agreed, the client then gives full approval. He or she is also shown any alterations to the narration script or the original narration script if it has been done at this stage, and gives approval.
- The narration is recorded.

- Final approval of the narration with the rest of the
programme or film is given by the client.
- The final master videotape (on-line edit) or show print of
a film is made. Any special video effects or film 'opticals'
are incorporated.
- Copies are made from the master.
- Copies are given to the client or distributed on his or her
behalf.

Needless to say, production schedules are not always as disci-
plined as this, and often the order in which things happen
changes according to circumstances. Flexibility within a
schedule is vital as you'll frequently find that its stages get
shifted around for reasons beyond anyone's control, and if
completion of a programme or a film by a certain deadline is
essential, then a flexible schedule gives you a fighting chance
of getting the show on the road on time.

The large videotape or film production

Once again this is perhaps a misnomer, in that what is actually
meant is more the complicated rather than the large. A 'large'
production of this nature might differ from the small one by
requiring actors or other performers to take part in some kind
of dramatisation, or it might need extensive location coverage
of a sporting or other event. In either case there would be a
need for more than one camera – possibly several – and, in the
case of videotape, an outside broadcast vehicle to provide
vision mixing and basic control on the spot. It also goes without
saying that the budget required for this production is considerably larger.

- The in-house team or chosen production company is briefed
by the originators of the programme or by the client.

Pre-production

- A scriptwriter and a director are called in. Together with
the producer, they will develop a treatment for the
production.
- The producer – or the production company's technical

31

producer or production manager – will do a 'recce' of
potential locations for the shoot.

- Recommendations for locations, as well as the treatment,
  a full costing and a production schedule are presented to
  the client. The client approves all these points and agrees
  the final budget.
- All relevant locations and studios are booked for shooting.
  Any necessary arrangements with the police, e.g. for
  street taping or filming or for the parking of OB and other
  support vehicles, should be made.
- If necessary, post-production facilities are booked.
- If actors are to be selected, a casting director or agency
  may have to be briefed at this stage. (Depending on the
  size of the production, this function may be performed by
  the director and other members of the production staff.)
- The script is written and a storyboard is prepared.
- The client is presented with the script and storyboard. Any
  necessary alterations are made and approval is given.
- Casting for performers takes place.
- Rehearsals of performers begin, with the director.
- Any necessary camera crew and equipment are hired. The
  size of the production company will normally dictate how
  much or how little of all the required equipment and staff
  are already on hand. Apart from crew, though, here are
  just a few other elements to be considered: cameras;
  lighting; sound; portable generator; OB unit equipped for
  multicam (multi-camera) shoot; crew accommodation and
  transportation; location or studio catering; props;
  wardrobe; hair and makeup artistes; set builders; plus back-
  up crew like electricians, carpenters, etc. And that's just
  a short list of things to be arranged, booked and confirmed.
- Production manager ensures that all crew, performers,
  client representatives and any other interested parties are
  told precisely what's required of them, where they should
  be collected from, at what time their calls are, and any
  other pertinent information.

Production

- On-set and/or location rehearsals take place.
- Principal photography (shooting) takes place, both on location and in the studio.
- Graphics, 'opticals' and any other special visual effects that require time to produce are put in hand.
- Rostrum filming or taping is done.

Post-production

The post-production procedure follows much the same pattern for the large videotape or film production as it does for the small one. The only noticeable difference, perhaps, is that the large production will take a lot longer to edit than will the simple single-camera variety.

Once again, the schedule mapped out above is by no means gospel; many productions go about their business in a somewhat different order.

Slide–tape and multi-image programmes and modules

With slide–tape programmes and modules the size of the production does not really make much difference to the way in which you approach it. The only thing to remember of course is that the more projectors you use, the more slides you'll need, generally, and the more slides you need the longer it will take to produce them all. Other than that, though, the principles are the same, and production goes in something resembling the following order. (Please note that we do not talk about pre-production, production and post-production here; a slide–tape or multi-image show is 'in production' from the day it is briefed and confirmed.)

- The in-house team or production company is briefed by the originators or the client company.
- A scriptwriter is called in to be briefed. He or she then prepares a skeleton or draft script. (As slide–tape and multi-image tends to be rather more words-led than motion pictures are, treatments are not often produced as a preliminary stage.)
- Script is visualised (written description of how screen

images will look) by the producer, scriptwriter, visualiser, or a combination of the three. The producer will also prepare a production schedule, a detailed budget based on the script, and the written visualisation in detail. Storyboards are not always produced with slide–tape or multi-image as it is more difficult to describe in simple terms what the visualiser or producer has in mind for the screen, especially with large-format shows. However, many production companies do provide storyboards for slide–tape and, this being the case, one will be produced at this stage.

- Script, visualisation and/or storyboard, budget and production schedule are presented to the client. Any necessary alterations are made and approval is given.
- Research and selection of any necessary library stills are done.
- A photographer is booked if there is not one already on the production company's staff.
- Any graphics input for the programme is initiated and production gets under way.
- Location photography dates are arranged.
- The narration is recorded, plus any other original sound. This may be in the production company's own studio, or it may be done at a specialist AV sound studio elsewhere.
- Location photography takes place.
- The final soundtrack is completed, not necessarily in the same studio, as even small production companies have small 'mixing' studios where this work can be done. This process involves adding on music, sound effects, etc. and ensuring that one track on the tape at least is left clear for the electronic pulses that instruct the projectors.
- All studio photography (indoor) is done, covering such items as products, packs, other small, static objects.
- All rostrum camera photography (e.g. lith, duping, etc.) is completed.
- All slide mounting is completed.
- Slides are assembled on a large lightbox, in show order. At this stage there may be some write-on slides in a few places, awaiting the yet-to-be-finished final slide.
- The client previews the slides on the lightbox and listens to the soundtrack. Approval is given.

- The slides are loaded into trays.
- Programming takes place, with electronic pulses being placed on the final showtape and the slides placed in magazines.
- Any late slides – replaced up until now by write-ons – are dropped into the magazines in their correct places.
- All slides are cleaned, using hand polishing and compressed air, then replaced into the magazines.
- The client watches the whole programme through and gives final approval.
- Copies of the show are made, if required. In the case of smaller-format programmes, they can now be transferred to videotape via a multiplexer or projection method if that is to be the final playback medium. A large format show can be reprogrammed down to a smaller number of projectors once it has been shown at a conference or meeting. This can then be shown at smaller meetings in slide–tape format or can be transferred to videotape for mass circulation. Obviously both primary and secondary playback intentions must be made clear to the production company from the start, because certain provisions must be made during production – particularly where a large format show is to be reprogrammed to a small format, or if the show is to be transferred to videotape.

The small business meeting

With a small meeting of, say, a couple of hours' duration, with around three or four speakers presenting to an audience of up to around 100, and once again a small budget, there will be very little in the way of staging required of the production company. In the following example we're assuming that there is no set to be built – we'll use a presentation room as it stands, with the venue's own lighting, lecterns and seating, etc. There will just be slides, with no other medium to project, and the slide input will consist of one multi-image module plus some speaker-support slides. There will be no teleprompter; speakers will cue their slides by pressing the cue-light button on the lectern.

This all represents a fairly typical example of the small shows many production companies produce by the dozen every year, and form the mainstay of the audio-visual industry's bread and butter. With business theatre – if you want to get the terminology right – a show goes 'into production' when it is being prepared, and goes 'out' when it is actually at the venue in rehearsal or performance. If it is going to travel to more than one venue it will be called a roadshow, and the crew and performers will be touring the show, but this example assumes that there is only one show in one venue. The larger breed of business theatre event is described later.

- In-house team or production company is called in by originators or client company. An overall brief, production schedule and budget are agreed, and preferred venues are decided on.
- Venues are recce'd and the most preferable booked. Any necessary equipment is hired and/or checked.
- A scriptwriter is called in and, together with the producer, takes a fuller brief from the client.
- The writer and producer create a treatment for the module, and probably a draft script as well. These are presented to the client, necessary changes are made and then approval is given.
- The module goes into production (see section on slide–tape and multi-image, page 33).
- The client presents the production company either with their own drafts of speeches, detailed notes from which the scriptwriter can work, or tape recordings of conversations between speakers and writer outlining the needs of each presentation.
- The scriptwriter prepares a draft of each speech and presents it back to the clients. They make any necessary changes and give approval.
- The speech scripts are visualised for speaker-support slide material and the visualisations shown to the client. The client makes any necessary alterations and gives approval.
- Speaker-support slides go into production (as for slide–tape or multi-image, except that there is no sound input).
- Once most of the slides are ready and the soundtrack for the module has been done, the client is invited to the production company's premises for a preview. This takes the form of a stagger-through rehearsal (although not at

the venue) of the speeches. Some production companies will provide a trained actor or stage director to coach the speakers at this point, helping them to get their messages over more effectively. The client will also preview the programmed module, although there may still be some late slides temporarily replaced by write-ons. This is the last opportunity speakers will have to make changes to their scripts and speaker-support slides.

- Finalisation of the module and speaker-support slides takes place.
- All equipment is packed. Speaker-support slides and the module, all programmed in show order, are packed too.
- All hardware and software are transferred to the venue. The crew (probably only a few people) do the 'get-in' and rig the equipment.
- The crew performs a technical rehearsal to ensure that all cues are on time and that everything is running smoothly.
- The speakers join in and a full rehearsal takes place, with the speakers running through their presentations several times if time permits.
- The show takes place.
- The crew performs the 'get-out', loads all the hardware and software and returns to base.

Perhaps it may sound repetitive but, once again, not all productions will run to this exact pattern, especially if the lead-time between briefing and show day is short. But in an ideal world, the above would probably allow a comfortable production period with plenty of time for everyone's performance to be polished and perfected.

The large business theatre event

Here we can really go mad for a few moments and take an example which includes all the fun of the fair. We assume that this show is to be a roadshow, so the set needs to be flexible enough in construction – and strong enough – to be rebuilt four or five times on tour. Music for the show will be specially composed and recorded; there will be dancers, properly choreographed; there will be short dramatisations which will require a cast of actors. In addition there will be a multi-image

37

rig of at least twenty-one projectors showing several modules; there will be speaker-support slides programmed over nine of those projectors; and there will also be projected videotape or film. A grand spectacular in true 1970s style, perhaps; however, shows of this magnitude are still commissioned and produced. They may cost a few corporate arms and legs, but you can't beat one of these if you really want to impress your audience.

- A production company is invited to take the show on. It is only in very rare circumstances that an in-house production department – no matter how efficient – should tackle a large spectacular like this; it is highly specialised work and should be left to those who specialise in it.
- Preferred venues are selected, a recce is done of each and a final selection is made. With client approval, firm bookings are made for each.
- The producer, scriptwriter and director spend time with the client researching the precise aims and requirements of the show.
- The producer, scriptwriter, production manager and director devise a production schedule, theme, treatment and running order for the show. This is then presented to the client, any necessary adjustments made and approval given.
- A set design is commissioned, produced and presented to the client. Pending client approval, the construction of the set is started.
- The scriptwriter prepares scripts of all live stage work, e.g. lyrics for songs, dramatisations, stand-up entertainers' sections, etc. These are presented to the client and approved.
- A casting director or agency is hired and briefed.
- A musical composer and a choreographer are hired and briefed. They begin their respective jobs immediately.
- Any celebrity or special guest speaker required is contacted and booked.
- Scripts and storyboards of the modules and VT or film inserts are done. These are presented to the client, any necessary alterations done and approved.
- Modules and VT or film inserts go into production (see

slide–tape/multi-image and VT/film sections respectively, pages 33 and 28).

- Road crew, stage crew, rigging and other technical crew are booked and confirmed for the tour by the production manager.
- All necessary equipment is booked and confirmed (over and above the production company's own equipment). Transportation for this and the set is booked. Carnet formalities and other documentation are completed if the show is going to a foreign country.
- Accommodation for crew and performers is booked at all venues. Their transportation is also arranged and booked.
- Casting for actors and dancers is done and the chosen people hired.
- A demonstration tape of the music is recorded and played to the client. Pending approval, the full recording of the music takes place.
- The choreography is described to the client and, pending approval, this is finalised. Dancers begin rehearsals.
- Actors and any other performers begin rehearsals. (Note that both the dance and the acting rehearsals are likely to take place in a draughty church hall, hired for the occasion by the production company.)
- Clients' speeches are drafted, approved and visualised.
- Speaker-support slides are produced (see slide–tape and multi-image section, page 33, but bear in mind that these do not include any sound).
- Speakers preview their slides at the production company's premises, make any necessary alterations and approve. All modules and VT or film inserts are shown and, pending client approval, are finalised.
- Speakers rehearse their presentations with their slides at the production company's premises, with a trained coach or the show director.
- Key personnel at the production company have one final progress meeting to ensure all components of the show are ready to go.
- The set, staging, lighting, projection, sound and all other equipment is assembled. All software is assembled too. All sound for the show (with the exception of VT or film inserts) is incorporated into one master tape. Also on this

tape will be any incidental music (other than walk-in/walk-out music) plus announcements, etc. The tape, plus a spare copy for luck, is carefully packed with the other software. Everything is then loaded into vehicles and despatched to the first venue.

- The production crew arrives at the first venue.
- The equipment and the other crews arrive at the first venue. Get-in takes place.
- All crews work hard to build the set and rig sound, lighting, projection and other equipment. This sometimes involves at least one all-night stint for the crew and sometimes two – but they're used to it!
- All speakers and performers arrive at the first venue.
- The crew – and only the crew – have a full technical rehearsal.
- All actors, dancers and other performers rehearse, not necessarily in show order.
- All speakers rehearse, not necessarily in show order.
- A full dress rehearsal takes place with all speakers and performers. The show will be run through completely, in order. If there is time, it will go through a complete run-through for a second time.
- The first performance of the entire show takes place.
- The crew strikes the set, packs up the equipment, does the get-out and loads everything back on to the vehicles.
- All crew, speakers, performers and equipment transfer to the next venue.
- The crew does the get-in at the next venue.
- The crew re-assembles the set and rigs all lighting, sound, projection and other equipment.
- The crew holds a full technical rehearsal.
- A top-and-tail rehearsal is held for all speakers and performers.
- The second performance of the entire show takes place.

. . . and so on, all the way around the tour venues.

Well, for the very last time it must be said that the above schedule does not contain any hard and fast rules and that it can only represent a very rough guide to the plan of attack for a large business theatre event. Depending on a number of factors, the order will change quite substantially, but in overall terms production is normally approached in roughly the above order.

Please note the following abbreviations throughout the dictionary section:
    ST   Slide–tape
    BT   Business theatre (conferences)
    VT   Videotape

accelerated motion (*film*) when you want to create a 'speeded-up' **sequence** in a film, you might imagine that all you have to do is tweak up the projector. Wrong; it's the other way round. You slow down the film camera, so that when the film is put through the projector at normal speed, the **action** looks faster. Accelerated motion is thus decelerated camera speed.

    See also **slow motion**

acoustic flat (*VT, film, BT*) a piece of scenery or a stage **flat** which is designed to deaden sound rather than reflect it and bounce it off. Usually the flat will have been painted with a special substance or will be covered in a specifically sound-deadening material.

acoustic perfume (*sound*) *See* **white noise**

acoustics (*sound, BT*) sound itself, or at least the science of it. In the context of business theatre, you'll often hear reference to acoustics when talking about the quality of sound within a **venue**. If the room has a high ceiling and plenty of marble or other hard surfaces everywhere, generating a lot of echo, it has 'bad acoustics'. This is because any sound generated through **speakers** will bounce about all over the place. A room with a low ceiling, lots of carpet, curtains and other sound-deadening materials will have 'good acoustics'; sound will be easy to control. The other occasion on which you might hear the word 'acoustic', in the singular, is in reference to musical instruments.

42

An acoustic guitar, for example, is one which is not plugged into anything; an acoustic piano is the old-fashioned type that is not assisted by technology. So, you have acoustic instruments, as opposed to electric or electronic ones.

action (*VT*, *film*) the actual physical activity which takes place in a programme or film. However the word is more commonly associated with what directors say on **set** or **location** when they want the performers to perform. With videotape, where the sound and vision are in one machine, the director will tell the camera operator to get going first. With film, where sound and vision are recorded on different machines, the director will tell sound to start fractionally before the camera. Then comes the magic word – 'Action!'

ad lib (*VT*, *film*, *BT*, *sound*) what good speakers do well and bad speakers get so wrong it sends audiences to sleep and drives producers and crews to the brink of suicide. For a speaker with programmed slide-support, to ad lib is all right provided he or she returns to the place in the **teleprompter** script where he or she left off. If possible, the speaker should warn the **crew** that an ad lib is likely to take place at a given point; this is likely to emerge during **rehearsal**. Otherwise, if there's no warning, you'll have the producer and programmer frothing at the mouth searching for some non-existent slide **cue**. (Ad libbing is also known as going **off-script**.) With videotape programmes, films and audio tracks, the only place where you're likely to come up against ad libbing is in **interviews**. Scripted interviews tend to sound phoney; ad libbed interviews, with interviewees speaking in their own words, are infinitely more believable. You just need to make sure everyone knows what questions will be asked beforehand, so no-one's caught on the hop without an answer.

ADO (*VT*) one of the many machines on the market – this one made by Ampex – which create videotape **digital effects**. This particular job can produce most of the **animation** effects and fancy tricks anyone's likely to need to make a truly jazzy videotape programme.

aerial shot (*ST*, *VT*, *film*) any still or motion picture which is

A

shot from the air. Usually this is taken to mean photography done from a helicopter or fixed-wing aircraft, but sometimes when the budget's tight you can get away with sticking the camera on a **cherrypicker** or on the top of a high building. With a good **zoom** lens, the effect of movement from on high can sometimes be very effective.

afternoon bath (*film*) when you're making a film, the usual procedure is that the exposed film is processed overnight. The procedure of developing the film is referred to as the bath. When you're in a hurry, you forget the overnight bit and ask the processing laboratory to do an afternoon bath. That way, with any luck, you'll get your **rushes** back the same day.

air (*ST, VT*) for air read space. With slides, to leave 'plenty of air' around an image or word on the **artwork** for a slide means to leave plenty of clear uncluttered space. In the VT context it means much the same – lots of blank space surrounding the focal point on screen.

all singing, all dancing (*BT*) a tongue-in-cheek term for a theatrically splendid business theatre event. Sometimes, of course, big presentations *do* include some singing and dancing. The term is also used to differentiate the more entertaining parts of a presentation, such as little comedy skits, songs and so on, from the more serious business elements.

ambient light (*VT, film, ST*) the existing light on **location**, before the **crew** starts flicking switches. This can be natural daylight or existing electric light sources.

ambient noise (*sound*) the curse of the **location** sound recordist. This represents all the apparently insignificant little rustlings, tweetings and thumpings our own ears take for granted. Through the powerful, sensitive microphones used today, the ring of a distant phone can sound like a fire engine, a passing car like a high-revving tractor, and faraway human voices like a swarm of bees. Even fluorescent lights, so harm-lessly illuminating our offices and homes, give off an irritating hum that can spoil a **soundtrack**. **Interviews** done on location should always be carried out in a small room, with fluorescent

A

lights turned off and telephones off the hook. Suitable background noise, to give a realistic 'on the spot' effect, can always be recorded separately and added on to the **master** tape in the **studio**. That way, an interviewee's voice will not suddenly get drowned by a slamming door or the rattle of the tea lady's trolley.

amplifier (*sound*) a machine which increases sound level. The signal going into the machine is amplified – or enlarged if you like – electronically. The output is many, many times louder than what went in.

anamorphic lens (*film*) have you ever wondered how on earth those tremendously wide-screened pictures you sometimes see at the movies can actually get through a normal-sized movie projector? Well, that's where the anamorphic lens system comes in handy. When the movie is shot, the lens compresses the wide aspect down to standard-size film. Then, when the movie is projected, a complementary system re-establishes it as wide-screen in the cinema. Clever stuff.

anchor (*VT*, *film*, *BT*) an American TV term for a **presenter**. In the original usage it means the studio presenter or newsreader who stays put (hence anchored) while handing over to outside reporters for on-the-spot coverage of news or other events. In this business we use the term when we do an in-company news programme, in much the same way as a broadcast version. In business theatre, you'll sometimes hear the term when there is a central, usually professional, presenter who comperes a conference and introduces speakers, **modules**, coffee break, lunch, tea, etc. You'll also hear anchor-man and anchor-woman.

animatic (*VT*, *film*) a term from the wonderful world of advertising, although in theory it could apply to any videotape or film project. Rather than show a client the raw **storyboard** of a production as it is drawn, the production people will **shoot** each section of it, in order, on videotape or film. This way clients can see the drawn images from the storyboard on a TV screen, which makes it look more like the finished article. Combined with this will be either the **demo** of a **soundtrack**,

A

or possibly the finished sound, in all the appropriate places. If it is a videotape version, it is called an animatic; if shot on film, it's sometimes referred to as a film storyboard. Another way of providing a halfway house between storyboard and finished production is to make a **photomatic**.

animation (*VT, ST, film*)
(1) videotape animation is not unlike that of **slide–tape**. However there is one major difference; whereas the effect of moving and playing about with images on slide necessitates a lot of slide production and elbow grease, **digital effects** on tape can be created by hitting a few buttons. Expensive, for sure; but with the many magic machines available in video studios today, in just a few hours you can make programmes jump up and down quite spectacularly.
(2) slide–tape animation is the effect of moving an image around on screen. To do this you need quite a few **projectors**; three is the basic minimum. With three, you can achieve the effect of a **logo** or other design rotating, although it may seem a bit jerky. Six or more projectors do the job better. Other slide–tape animation effects include moving an image in a spiral, up and down, from one side to the other, diagonally, and out from the middle of the screen. Also, by building up parts of a whole image (each bit on a separate slide), a **multi-projector rig** can make an image appear to start from a pinprick, then grow into a large object; or, the other way round, you can make a image disappear gradually. These are just some of the animation effects possible with slide–tape; there are many more!
(3) a more high-falutin' word for cartoon in the film context. People in the business don't mind referring to the Disney brand of animation as cartoons, but might get a bit upset if you were to so label a serious 'art' animated film. The word can also be used to describe clay or other models or puppets, filmed in **stop motion** to mimic movement.

answerprint (*film*) the first full copy of your film, after the editing has been done. It's the intermediate stage between the **cutting copy**, which is the one with which you can play about with scissors, and your **show copy**, which is the final product. The point of the answerprint is to reveal the film in its entirety without any editing hiccups. However, there will still be work to be done on quality, grading and colour; once these have been adjusted and commented on, the laboratory can then produce the final show copy.

applebox (*VT*, *film*) not a real applebox, nor is it an orange crate, as it is also called from time to time. However it is of a similar size and shape, and is used either to raise props up, or to raise short actors up, so they'll look respectively higher or taller to the camera.

arc (*VT*, *film*, *BT*, *ST*) a light, and a very high-powered one at that. Arcs are used either inside **projectors** or on their own in **studios**, and are powered by two carbon rods with an electrical discharge between them.

arc out (*VT*, *film*) camera lenses are pernickety – at least most camermen will assure you they are. They don't see things quite the way our eyes do. For example, if a performer walks in a straight line from **camera right** to **camera left**, the lens will see it as if he had veered drunkenly towards the camera at the halfway point. So, if the **director** wants the performer to appear to walk in a straight line from one side of the camera to another, he'll tell the performer to 'arc out'. The actor then walks in a curved line from one side to the other, veering away from the lens at mid-point, and the finished effect will appear dead straight.

arrangement (*sound*) a term used in music recording. The arrangement of a piece of music consists of the entire musical score. Nowadays many composers can't write music down on paper and are not trained to work out which instruments should play what, what harmonies the singers should do, and so on. So somebody else takes the basic idea, the kernel of the composition, and writes out suitable parts for each instrument and singer. That's an arrangement. Of course, some composers can and do create their own arrangements and when this happens it's likely that they will be credited for both, i.e. 'Music composed and arranged by . . .'

arranger (*sound*) the person who arranges a piece of music.

A

This can either be the composer of the music, or someone else who is hired in to do the job after the composer has created his or her original musical idea.

See also **arrangement**

artwork (*ST, VT, film*) the original drawing, diagram or words which make up a **slide** or a **caption**. Artwork for slides or captions has to be painfully accurate and well positioned, otherwise it will appear crooked when photographed, filmed or **vision-mixed** into a videotape. Photography of artwork is normally done under a **rostrum camera**. Usually the paper on which the artwork is done is pinned through its own special holes to the drawing board by means of a clip, to keep it straight and level and within the right **frame** area for filming or photography. This is called pin registration. Artwork can be an original drawing, instant dry lettering, **typesetting** which is cut up into appropriate strips and stuck down, or a combination. When a **build-up** is required, layers of clear plastic – **cells** – are used. Each layer represents one section of the build-up, and the appropriate letters and drawings for each part are stuck down on one cell after another. When the artwork is photographed, each cell goes under the camera separately, all registered, of course, so you can't see the joins.

ashcan (*BT*) a theatrical light located in a compartment in the **footlights**. It consists of an open reflector, two 1-kilowatt bulbs, and a frosted-glass diffuser to complete the effect.

aspect ratio (*VT, film, ST, BT*) the ratio of the height to the width of an image. In the case of videotape, you're talking about the ratio of the picture on screen; this is 3 to 4; 35 mm slides have an aspect ratio of 2 to 3. We sometimes talk about aspect ratio when referring to the shape of **multi-image** screens, too.

assemble edit (*VT*) a videotape editing term. It's the function of re-recording all the necessary sections of tape you choose from the various different tapes you've shot, on to one blank tape, in the order you want. This will form the final programme. **Insert editing**, on the other hand, is replacing any segment on ιhe final tape with another of the same length from one of your origination tapes.

audience (*all*) in the case of business theatre, your audience is right there before your very eyes – a group of people to be impressed and motivated (usually), as well as entertained and inspired. Quite a responsibility. But at least with a live audience you can judge their reaction to the presentation you make, there and then. With the audience involved with videotape programmes, films, small slide–tape shows, and sound, you can't see them, which is sometimes unnerving. But whether you can see them or not, it is vital that the target audience for any presentation is studied carefully, and that every millisecond of a presentation is created in the best possible way to make the desired effect on the audience concerned.

audio (*all*) another word for sound. The audio content of any programme is the **soundtrack** – all parts which can be heard and not necessarily seen. The word is used on **scripts** sometimes; the visual content will be described on the left-hand side of the page, entitled 'video', and the words, **sound effects** and music preferences will be detailed on the right, under 'audio'. The more modern way of entitling such scripts is by using 'vision' and 'sound'.

audition (*all*) means exactly the same as it does in Hollywood, only in our business the casting couches and other clichés have been replaced by hard-working, business-like producers and clients. Actors, **voice overs**, dancers and other performers who work in our business may not find it as artistically satisfying as true show-business, but they certainly like the money and regular work. In a small- to medium-sized production, auditioning artists and other performers is normally done by the **producer** and client. For very large **shows**, a **casting director** will sometimes be employed just for the purpose.

Autocue (*ST, VT, film*) a trade name for one of the **tele-prompter** devices in common use. As this was one of the first such systems to be created, and has been around for a long time, the name is often mistakenly used to describe other

49

AV

people's machines as well. But Autocue *is* only a trade name, along with **QTV**, Portaprompt, and others.

AV (*ST*, *BT*) stands for audio-visual; probably the most abused term in the whole of this business. Correctly speaking, *any* presentation involving the use of sound and pictures simultaneously is an audio-visual presentation. However, in common usage, AV usually means **slide–tape**, **multi-image**, or any other combination of slides and a pre-recorded **soundtrack**. In business theatre, we refer to AVs when we mean self-contained slide–tape **modules**, as opposed to **speaker-support** sections. Similarly, we refer to 'AV links' when we mean a few slides with music to allow one speaker to get down off the stage and the next to get in place for his or her speech.

See also **multi-vision, tape–slide**

B

baby (*VT*, *film*) as the name suggests, a small **spotlight** of 750 watts. It is useful to light small areas within a short distance.

baby kicker (*or* **baby pup**) (*VT*, *film*) a baby-sized **key light**. *See also* **pup**

baby legs (*VT*, *film*) a small low-level **tripod** to hold up a camera.

baby pup (*VT*, *film*) *see* **baby kicker**

backcloth (*or* **background**) (*VT*, *film*, *BT*) a suitably-decorated piece of cloth or item of scenery that creates the desired atmosphere behind performers.

background colour (*ST*, *VT*, *BT*) the colour behind an image on screen. Usually this applies to **graphics** or **word slides**. With slides, it is possible to photograph the image with the background colour already in place. However, it is more common to shoot the graphics or words on **lith**, put that in one projector and project a plain background colour from another machine. The words or figures on the lith will **burn out** of the background colour. With graphics on videotape it is often possible to add a background colour by using a special effects machine, which can generate pretty well any colour you like at the touch of a button.

background sound (*sound*, *VT*, *film*) the noises you hear in the background when someone is interviewed outside a studio, e.g. traffic, other voices, etc. The real thing is called **ambient noise**, but to get a good **location** audio interview you're better to stick your interviewee in a quiet room with no ambient noise. Then you can tape the background noise separately in the

B

environment concerned and **mix** it with the voice **track** later in the studio – if you want to. The reason for doing this is so you can regulate the amount of background noise; the real thing can and often does drown out the interviewee's voice just at the wrong moment. And the true cheat can even use ready-made **soundtracks** of street noise, cocktail party chatter, etc., to provide the right ambience without the hassle. The picture does become a bit more complicated when you have to deal with background sound on a filmed or videotaped interview, largely because you can't 'cheat' in the way you do with audio only. The most efficient way of reducing the undesirable effects of background noise here is by using a high-quality **directional microphone** which picks up the sound it's pointed at and not too much else.

backing (*sound*) a musical term. Backing consists of all the peripheral music – instruments and vocals – that supports the lead singer or instrument. Hence backing vocals, backing singers, etc.

backing copy (*or* **back-up copy**) (*all*) whenever you produce a finished copy of a videotape, film, soundtrack or slide–tape programme, it's a wise precaution to make another one for luck. Sometimes, of course, **budget** is too restricted to allow this. But, budget restrictions or no, it's worth it. All it takes is for someone to spill a cup of coffee or forget their briefcase in a taxi, and a lot more of the budget will have been wasted. A back-up or backing copy is a valuable safeguard against the powers of fate.

backing track (*sound*) the recorded version of **backing**. Very often in music recording the backing track – with all the supporting instrumental and vocal parts – will be recorded before the main singer or instrument performs. And the backing, too, is often put down in sections; brass instruments, wood instruments, guitars and drums, backing vocals, etc. Using a **multi-track** recording machine, each section is recorded separately. Then, when the main voice or instrument has to be done, the singer or musician concerned listens to the backing track through his or her headphones and sings or plays along with it. Finally, all the various tracks are put together during the **mix-down**.

back projection (*BT*, *VT*, *film*)
(1) let's start with business theatre. With back projection, you put projectors behind a translucent screen, with the audience on the other side. You then turn the slides round back to front in the projectors and project them through the screen. The advantages of back projection over **front projection** are that you can project with a higher level of ambient light in the room, you can create a bigger image in a room with a low ceiling and, of course, the audience can't see or trip over a large projector rig at the back of the room they're sitting in.
(2) with film or videotape you'll sometimes use back projection if you need to shoot a scene with actors against an exotic background. Using the same technique as with business theatre, only with film and film projector, the actors can perform in front of, say, a tropical beach with waves crashing down on it, all inside a studio. Perhaps the best-remembered use of this technique was in older movies where actors would stare lovingly into each others' eyes while driving their car down a leafy lane. The actors and the car – or a mock-up of a car – would be in the studio; the leafy lane would be back-projected film.

backstage (*BT*) anywhere behind the **stage** and/or **set** in a business theatre production. Comes from entertainment theatre usage, but, whereas in a theatre, backstage is likely to mean comfortable dressing rooms where the performers entertain friends and fans after a show, in business theatre you're more likely to encounter miles of cables and ceiling-high stacks of equipment.

back-to-back productions (*or* **piggy-back productions**)
(*VT*, *film*, *sound*) back-to-back or piggy-back efforts basically save clients' money. They come about when a **crew** is going on **location** somewhere expensive. Often it will be found that if a crew is going to, say, Hong Kong, another client will wish to have some **footage** or tape shot in the same place. So, while the crew is out there, they will shoot both the original client's work, plus that of the other, thus saving both clients a bit of money on fares, accommodation, etc. This is equally applicable

to stills photographers shooting on behalf of **slide–tape** clients, and even to feature film productions.

bar chart (*VT*, *film*, *ST*) a way of illustrating different amounts – money, turnover, etc. – on a **graphic slide** or **sequence**. Each amount is represented by a horizontal bar of solid colour, in proportion to its neighbours. A visually simple and effective way of comparing figures on screen.

Barco (*VT*) the trade name of a type of **video projector**. It can be used for both **front projection** or **back projection** and will either project videotape recordings or, if plugged into a **CCTV** camera, whatever the camera picks up.

barn doors (*VT*, *film*) any fully-operational light will throw its beam roughly in the direction in which it is pointed. Barn doors are flaps which can be adjusted over the beam so that its effect can be altered in a variety of different directions. Smaller lights will often have two barn doors, operating on a horizontal basis; larger lights will have four barn doors, one on each side of a square casing.

barney (*or* **blimp**) (*film*) a padded casing that encloses a camera. This might be used during shots of a quiet, intimate scene; the effect of a barney is to deaden the sound of the camera's innards in operation. A 'self-blimped' camera is one which has a sound-proof casing built in. There is also such a thing as a heater barney, which – predictably enough – keeps the camera cosy and fully operational during **location** work in chilly weather.

barrel (*VT*) in a studio it's often necessary to hang lights from the ceiling. A barrel is a metal tube on which lights are so hung.

barricuda (*VT*) a telescopic device which supports a light at a great height. It's made from several lengths of metal pole.

basher (*VT*, *film*) a floodlight, on the small side. Its power ranges from 200 to 500 watts.

bath (*film*) the fluid, and the container, in which film is processed.

BCU (*VT, film, ST*) stands for big close up.
    See also **shot lengths**

B

beanstalk (*VT, film*) often lighting has to be pretty high up, especially on **location**. A beanstalk is a platform which rises up to about 20 feet, allowing **crew** to put lights up in high places.

bearding (*VT*) a hiccup in video reproduction. It occurs when the black tones overspill into the white areas on screen.

best boy (*VT, film*) a polite euphemism for someone who might consider him or herself as a glorified go-fer. This person assists either the **key grip** or the **gaffer**.

Betacam (*VT*) a comparatively recent addition to the range of different videotape formats. Betacam is only ½ an inch wide, like **VHS**, but through refined technology provides very much higher quality when used as the initiation medium. The quality is, some say, even better than that of BVU or **High Band**, although this is of course a matter of opinion. The advantage of Betacam is that, being smaller than High Band, its equipment is somewhat lighter and easier to use. A popular way to create programmes using Betacam – or High Band for that matter – is to shoot the original material on the smaller format and then transfer the whole lot to **1-inch** tape for editing. Using the larger format only for editing allows you the flexibility and leeway of the 1-inch size where you really need it, without the expense of carting it around to shoot all the original material. And the quality of Betacam (or High Band) is more than good enough for the sort of non-broadcast work involved in this business.

Betamax (*VT*) one of the popular videotape **cassette** formats, made by the Japanese firm Sony. Along with **VHS**, this is a format for home use or for very small audiences. The cassettes are marginally smaller than VHS.

billyboy dolly (*VT, film*) a **dolly** which can cope with the

B

hardest of assignments. It's a particularly tough type of dolly with pneumatic wheels, so that its movement doesn't interfere with sound recording.

binstick (*film*) a stick or pole, made of wood or metal, that hangs over the **bin** during the film editing. On this you can hang **clips** or short sequences of film so they're immediately to hand.

bin (*film, sound, BT*)
(1) during film editing the 'bin' contains complete sequences ready to be edited in. It's just a suitably sized and shaped container.
(2) nickname for very powerful **speakers**, used to generate atmosphere at business-theatre **venues**. The most powerful of these can transmit sound that convinces the audience they're standing right by Concorde at take-off.

bird (*VT*) a nickname for a satellite which you use to transmit international TV programming. Used as a verb, the act of so doing. In the non-entertainment side of the business, the only likely place you'll come across satellite work is in a **DBS teleconference**.

black crush (*VT*) a way of bringing down the black level on screen so as to create a more favourably cheerful background for **captions**.

black-edge generator (*VT*) sometimes **captions** on screen don't seem to stand out too well. A black-edge generator will provide a black edging round the characters, making them more prominent.

blackout (*BT*)
(1) when the screen is totally black, without images on it.
(2) when all the lighting in a **venue** is **killed** and you're in total darkness. Usually happens immediately prior to a dramatic visual effect.

blacks (*BT*) the black bits of **flat** or cloth used to hide all

56

the paraphernalia **backstage** – or to camouflage anything the audience shouldn't see.

blimp (*film*) *see* **barney**

blind wipe (*VT*) a **wipe** effect that resembles the action of a Venetian blind. Through the appearance and disappearance of a series of lines running parallel to one side of the screen, you wipe from one picture to the next. Pretty, provided it isn't used too often within a programme.

blonde (*VT, film*) a quartz-iodine light with 2 kilowatts of power.

bloop (*sound*) a method of covering up a join in a sound tape. You can either use 'blooping ink' (a thick fluid) or 'blooping tape'.

boat truck (*VT, film, BT*) a trolley, with wheels, on which bits of equipment, **flats**, parts of a **set** and so on are transported.

bon-bon (*BT*) a **spotlight** with 2 kilowatts of power. It's used to throw light on to one specific area, often the face of a performer.

boom (*sound, film, VT*) a long arm, usually attached to the camera or sound unit, which holds a microphone at the business end. When you're shooting a **sequence** on **location** or in the studio and you're not using **neck mikes** or **lapel mikes**, the **mike** boom will hover overhead out of the camera's view, but near enough to the performers to pick up the sound.

boomy (*sound*) if you think of someone with a booming voice, you'll probably remember that his or her lowest sounds – although not as shrill as the high notes – remind you of an aircraft breaking the sound barrier, or an explosion. With sound recording or reproduction, low loud sounds within a **track** can get distorted, which creates a similar effect and makes them 'boom' through the **speakers**. Hence 'boomy' sound.

boring (*all*) a danger to which everyone in our business should develop a violent allergy. With **broadcast** sound and television, those responsible have large, open-minded audiences to answer to, and boring programmes get taken off as soon as the ratings dip. However, business or training audiences don't normally have a choice about whether or not to switch off their programmes or walk out of performances. And there is a tendency among companies and people who produce non-broadcast industrial material to forget that bored audiences – even if you've nailed their feet to the floor – will not absorb very much information if they find a programme dull. Long **sequences** of **talking heads**, endless unbroken facts and figures, or even too many of the Chairman's well-chosen philosophies might be fascinating to management. But to avoid boredom, which wastes everyone's time and money, you must consider the audience's point of view. You've got to produce **shows** that will attract and hold the audiences' attention, that will speak their language and satisfy their needs, while simultaneously getting over the messages in question.

box (*VT, sound*)
(**1**)   in big videotape and/or television studios, the controls and controlling individuals sit in the 'box' – a sound-proofed gallery overlooking the studio floor.
(**2**)   in sound studios the 'box' is the sound-proofed room where the performers perform. This is also called the sound booth.

brace (*BT*) an implement which holds something up, in this case scenery or another part of the **set**. It's usually a piece of wood or a metal bar. The brace weight, not surprisingly, is a heavy lump of metal which strengthens the purpose of the brace. Braces and brace weights are very useful, but also easy to trip over. Business-theatre **producers** are well advised to get someone to put white **gaffer tape** all over such pieces of equipment so no-one trips over them while the auditorium is in near-darkness during a **show**.

brace weight (*BT*) *see* **brace**

bracketing (*ST, BT*) a still photographic technique used in **multi-image** work. One of the more dramatic effects you can create on screen is to start with a very dark outlook to an image, almost as if it is in shadow, and gradually make it appear lighter and lighter until it is in full view. This is an especially useful trick when you're creating a **reveal**. It is done by placing the object to be photographed in a studio in front of the camera; you then shoot a series of pictures, each time altering the light setting on the camera or altering the studio lighting slightly. The resulting sequence of stills is then projected in order.

breakthrough (*VT*) with different types of electrical machinery running side by side in close physical proximity, signals from one system can find their way from one to another. This is called breakthrough.

bridle (*BT*) part of the stage equipment. A bridle is a kind of **brace** that supports the ropes, which in turn support the stage **drapes**.

brief (*all*) the document, or conversation, which determines the background, audience, objectives, and other requirements of a **production** in embryo. The brief must be put together by whoever is commissioning a production, so that the production team is able to meet its requirements accurately. Often the person or group of people commissioning a production will need to discuss their requirements with the production team, in order to pinpoint the exact specification. A good, full and thorough brief is essential to the successful production of any film, **programme** or **soundtrack**.

broad (*VT, film, BT*) a small floodlight, shaped like a box.

broadcast (*VT*) a broadcast programme is one which is, or is intended to be, transmitted out to an unknown and unseen audience; in other words, television or radio programmes that you receive at home. This is as opposed to non-broadcast programmes, sometimes called **narrowcast**, which are made and shown or transmitted to specific, non-domestic audiences.

broadcast quality (*or* **broadcast standard**) (*VT*) any video-tape programme which is of a sufficiently high technical standard to be transmitted out on television. This normally means that the videotape programme has been made on either **1-inch** or **2-inch** tape, although **BVU** is said to be of broadcast quality, too.

broadcast standard (*VT*) *see* **broadcast quality**

brute (*VT*, *film*) a light of between 15 and 22½ kilowatts in power. Can be focused.

BU (*ST*, *BT*) stands for **build-up**.

budget (*all*) as in most business enterprises, the amount of money available to spend on any given project. The source of much anxiety among producers, especially when exceeded!

build-up (*ST*, *VT*, *film*, *BT*) a sequence of **graphics** coming up on **screen**. This can be a series of words or phrases, as in **bullet points**; it can be figures; and it can also be parts of a chart, building up to a whole, as in the case of **bar charts** or **column charts**. With single-projector slides, the build-up will consist of a series of slides starting with one showing the first point to appear, followed by a second slide with the first and second points on it, followed by a third slide with points one, two and three, and so on, until you get to the last slide which has all the necessary points on it. When these slides are projected and **dissolved** through in sequence, it will look as though one point is coming up after another. When you have several projectors, each point can be on a different slide, although this is not always suitable. Obviously, it is important that the original **artwork** is designed in registered form, and shot properly on the **rostrum camera**, otherwise the projected effect will look jerky. With videotape, graphics build-ups can be generated electronically. It's also possible to create flat artwork and shoot it under camera in the same way as for slides; both film and videotape rostrum cameras are suitable for this. The term is sometimes abbreviated to **BU**.

bullet points (*VT*, *film*, *ST*) part of the **graphics** and **caption** world. When you have several verbal points to list on an **artwork** slide, be it for projection as a slide or for use on film

60

or videotape, you can arrange the phrases in bullet points. This means each phrase is preceded by an asterisk, dash, or other graphic symbol, and the list of bullet points is neatly arranged down the centre of the screen area.

B

burn out (*ST*) when the white image of words or figures projected on **lith** burn out of a background colour. It means that the white projected lith, being more powerful in light measurement terms, will be seen as white, despite there being another colour there. Projected lith graphic slides won't burn out of very pale colours, like light yellow.

busk (*all*) a general slang term, really, from the old French verb *busquer* (to seek one's fortune) or the Italian *buscare* (to prowl with dishonest intent). Nowadays, buskers are the entertainers who play in bus stations, Underground tunnels and cinema queues. The verb to busk has come to mean clever, creative improvisation when equipment or other circumstances have let you down. So, in this business a speaker might 'busk' part of a business theatre presentation if his or her teleprompt device fails; or a scriptwriter might 'busk' the writing of a passage in a script where there is less than enough information to substantiate the narration content. With luck, you won't hear this word too often . . .

BVU (*VT*) a videotape format. This is quite widely used for taping non-broadcast VT programmes, as the quality is quite reasonable and the cost of it is low when compared to **1-inch** or **2-inch**. BVU, also known as **High Band**, is officially supposed to be broadcast-standard tape; however very few broadcast programmes are made with it in Europe or the United States, anyway. It, like **Low Band**, is ¾-inch wide.

C

cable (*VT*) cable television, very popular in the USA, is now becoming increasingly visible in Europe. The main difference is that cable is transmitted down cables, or wires, which are plugged into TV sets rather as telephone connections are made, while **Broadcast** television is transmitted over the air waves to aerials on roofs.

cabtyre (*BT*) stage cable, packed around with thick rubber. The stage cable may also be stuck down with **gaffer tape**, in the hope that performers and **crew** won't trip over it.

CAD (*VT*) acronym for computer aided design. Using a special computer, it is possible to instruct the machine to create a graphics **animation** sequence, three-dimensional if required, with the only human input being one ordinary two-dimensional drawing or other piece of **artwork**. A UK example of this, at the time of writing, is the animation of the Channel Four television **logo**. You may also hear the expression CAD/CAM. The first part translates as above, and the second half stands for Computer Aided Manufacture – not an area that concerns this business very much, but a closely-related process nonetheless. Computer-aided design and manufacture, in this context, are more common in industry – for example, design and manufacture of motor car components, etc.

call (*VT, film, BT*)
(1) the noun is a rendezvous, appointment or deadline. So, if you're to **shoot** on **location** and you want everyone to be there by 9 am, they will all have a 9 o'clock call.
(2) as a verb, to call a **show** means to give out instructions to the **crew** over the **cans** while the show is in progress. Normally, this task falls to the **producer** or the **programmer**. The instruc-

62

tions include all lighting and sound **cues**, plus cues for film, videotape and slide projectionists, **teleprompt** operator, etc.

camera left (*VT*, *film*, *ST*) the direction as if you were looking through the lens of the camera, as opposed to stage left or right, which is the other way around.
See also **stage directions**

camera right *see* **camera left**

C

camera script (*VT*, *film*) the full script containing the **dialogue** and/or **narration**, plus detailed camera instructions for each **shot**. Also called shooting script or dope sheet.

cans (*BT*, *sound*) slang for headphones. In the recording studio, cans tend only to receive sound. However in business theatre the production **crew** will use **headsets** that also have a built-in microphone, so the **producer** can give them instructions and so that everyone can communicate back to him or her should a problem arise. These microphones are sensitive enough to pick up a whisper, so the crew can chat even when there is a **speaker** performing on stage.

cap gen (*VT*) acronym for caption generator. A machine which electronically generates and automatically records **captions** to be put on to a videotape programme.

captions (*VT*, *film*) originally, words superimposed over a picture. Now taken more generally to mean any words or **artwork** appearing in a moving picture. However, it's still used in its original sense as well. Captions or **credits** can roll, which means they come up as if they were rolling vertically up or down the screen, or they can crawl from right to left. (No doubt if the captions are in Arabic, they'd roll from left to right – a small point to remember in our global village . . .)

Caramate (*ST*) a small, self-contained unit, made by Kodak, that **back-projects** one **Carousel** of slides, accompanied by a synchronised soundtrack, on to its own little screen. The whole thing looks like a slightly clumsy TV set. Caramates have been immensely popular for a long time, being one of the most portable – and idiot-proof – systems of showing single-projector slide–tape programmes.

Carousel (*ST, BT*) many people use this as a term to refer to any rotary slide **magazine** and the system of projection that goes with it. However, it is a trade name belonging to the mighty Kodak.

car-park job (*VT, film, ST*) usually a short **sequence** that's left until last in a production, after the **crew** has finished shooting on **location**. If it's an **exterior** shot it can usually be done on a handy bit of local terrain like, for example, the production company's car park, so saving the client time and money by avoiding unnecessary extra location costs.

cart (*all*) abbreviation for **cartridge**.

cartridge (*all*) a closed package of tape with just one reel inside. Normally, cartridges operate on a loop principle, which means they'll go on playing the programme over and over again until you press a button to shut them up. Cartridges are used a lot in radio stations for commercials, station identifications, jingles and so on. This is because they don't have to be threaded up into tape players. They're also used for **sound effects** – most sound studios will have a library of **SFX** carts ready to incorporate into a production.

cassette (*all*) a closed package of either sound or videotape. Inside there is a take-up reel and a supply reel – the latter feeds the former. The thing that differentiates cassettes from cartridges is that they play the programme once only, and then have to be rewound.

cast (*VT, film, BT*)
(1) as a noun, the cast consists of all actors and extras performing in any given **production**. This does not normally include other performers such as presenters, reporters, company executives taking part, etc., as they only play themselves. The cast are performers who play the parts of others.
(2) as a verb, to cast means to select actors for the job in hand.

casting (*VT, film, BT, sound*) the act of choosing or selecting performers for a **production**.
See also **casting director**

casting director (*VT, film, BT*) the person who auditions and chooses the **cast** for a **production**. When budgets are small this job tends to be done by the director or producer, but when there is to be a large cast, a specialist can sort out the wheat from the chaff very efficiently. Many casting directors are **freelance**.

cat glass (*ST, VT, film*) the special grain-free screen material used when **back-projecting** one medium to transfer it to another, e.g. slide to videotape. For more complicated transfers see **multiplexer**.

CATV (*VT*) stands for community antenna television. It's a relatively new concept which allows a community of homes to receive TV down cables from a central antenna, which picks up **broadcast** signals and distributes them.

CCTV (*VT*) stands for closed circuit television. Basically, television that isn't going anywhere, just to a specified selection of **monitors** in a given space.

cell (*ST, film*) a piece of clear transparent plastic, used in **artwork** to create **build-ups**. Figures and numbers are normally stuck on to it. Several cells, appropriately numbered, will be used in a build-up, on a registration system. **Rostrum** photography is done part by part, with cells being added one at a time until the whole picture is complete. This is also the way in which cartoons are made.

changing bag (*film*) when you're changing film magazines in a camera, you've got to do it in the dark. Any light sneaking in can ruin the film. So the changing is done inside a lightproof bag, with much fumbling and groping. Quite alarming for the uninitiated to watch for the first time.

charlie bars (*VT, film*) small flaps which fit over the front of a light to disperse the beam.

chequerboard (*film*) a method of **cutting** negative film, and usually the preferred way of doing it because you can't see the joins. It is also the best way to prepare **opticals**.

cherrypicker (*ST, VT, film*) a type of mobile crane, with a platform or cage mounted on the top. These machines are rather like those used by people who repair broken street lights. In fact, although major television and film companies will probably have their own, smaller production companies have been known to hire cherrypickers from the local council. The idea is to put a camera up top, so you can get high up and move the thing around too. Big productions might use a cherrypicker to light a particularly tricky shot, but in the main it's a film, VT or stills-camera operator who gets the short straw. Not surprisingly, cameramen with vertigo problems will plead for a helicopter, but cherrypickers are a lot cheaper to hire and with a good **zoom** lens on the camera the result is almost as good as a low **aerial shot**.

Chinagraph pencil (*film, sound*) a trade name that has found its way into general terminology. It's normally made of light-coloured wax, sharpened well, and used to mark film or audio tape for **editing** or **cue**ing purposes.

Chinese (*VT, film*) horizontal slits created by adjusting the **barn doors** appropriately over a light.

chippie (*VT, film, BT*) nickname for a carpenter, who builds and constructs **sets**. In America, carpenters are sometimes called carps.

christmas tree (*VT, film*) a small trolley or cart used to lug lighting around. So-called as the equipment tends to get strung around it as do lights on a Christmas tree.

chromakey (*VT*) the American term for colour separation overlay.
   See also **CSO**

cinching (*VT, film, sound*) when tape or film is being wound on spools, sometimes the winding process is not uniform. This creates spaces within the layering on the spool – cinching.

Cinemascope (*film*) a type of film that gives a very wide picture. You need to use an **anamorphic lens** in order to project it. The **aspect ratio** of Cinemascope is 2.35 to 1, as opposed to TV, which is 4 to 3.

C

cinematographer (*film*) the most senior person in charge of photography. Sometimes called the **lighting cameraman**.

clapperboard (*or* **slate**) (*film*) a board on which details of each shot are written. It's then placed in front of the camera at the start of each shot so that the **editor** will be able to identify it easily. Lastly, a hinged section of the board is clapped down so that the sound it makes will allow full synchronisation between sound recording and film.

clip (*film*) a short length of film. Either used to describe the physical object, i.e. a length of film a few feet long, or else an excerpt shown from a longer production.

clock (*VT*) with a videotape programme, even a very short one, there will nearly always be a recorded countdown with the start of it. This is to allow an accurate timing of the start of the programme – especially necessary for television commercials, etc.

clogging (*VT*) what happens when bits of loose tape-coating get in between the tape that's being played and the sound or video **head** of the machine. The result is a partial loss of sound or picture.

closed circuit TV (*VT*) *see* **CCTV**

close-up (*VT*, *film*, *ST*) *see* **shot lengths**

cloud projector (*VT*, *film*, *BT*) a special light fitted with a device that moves or revolves. The result is the effect of clouds scudding across the sky – with a little theatrical licence, of course . . .

coding (*VT*) sometimes referred to as encoding. This is the process that takes place in order to transfer a colour video signal – known as RGB (red, green and blue, the primary video colours) – to one of the standard television formats for general viewing. Such formats are **PAL** in the UK, **NTSC** in the USA, **SECAM** in France.

C

colouration (*sound*) a term used to describe the way a **voice over** artiste speaks. Colouration is the character and the style in which the script is read. To add more colouration to a voice-over is to make it more lively, more vocally 'colourful'. To reduce colouration is to bring the voice down to a more business-like, serious style, rather like that of a **newsreader voice**.

colour bars (*VT*) a test signal that comes up on screen. Eight vertical bars, including – from left to right – white, yellow, cyan, green, magenta, red, blue, black.

colour conversion (*ST*) a **rostrum camera** process whereby words or figures in negative black and white on **lith** film are re-photographed to include colours and/or **special effects** like **neon**.
See also **lith**

colour separation overlay (*VT*) *see* **CSO**

colour synthesiser (*VT*) an electronic device which can produce instant colour on screen, either for **captions** or background, or both. Most machines can colour both in different colours, too.

column chart (*VT*, *film*, *ST*) falls within the area of **artwork** and **graphics**, although column charts can be computer generated. Very like a **bar chart**, except the bars run vertically. Used to illustrate different quantities on screen, often with each column in a different colour.

combined print (*film*) the first print of a film which has both vision and **soundtrack** on it. Also known as a married print.

comes down (*BT*) term switched from traditional theatre. A **show** comes down (ends) at a given time.
See also **goes up**

commentary (*VT*, *film*, *ST*, *sound*) although this word is often used as a synonym for a **narration**, this is not strictly correct. A commentary should be an *un*-scripted **voice-over**, with someone 'commentating' on a specific event.

C

compact cassette (*sound*) a small, handy-sized audio **cassette** most people play in their homes or cars.

compact VHS (*VT*) a very small videotape format. The actual **cassette** isn't much bigger than a **compact cassette** audio tape. It can either be played back on its own very small equipment, or, using a special adaptor, it can be played back on a standard **VHS** machine.

composer (*sound*) a person who writes tailor-made music for any production. Very effective, but expensive. The cheaper alternative is **library music**.

compressed air (*ST*) used to clean slides, removing tiny particles of dust and grit. Either comes in an aerosol spray or is piped from a tank.

computer generated (*VT*, *ST*) refers largely to **graphics** and **special effects**. With slides you can use a computer with a special graphics package to design **artwork** or **captions**. Then, through a special method, the image is photographed on 35 mm stills film and processed in the normal way. **Digital effects** – the fancy tricks you do with videotape – are similarly computer generated.

condenser mike (*sound*) also known as an electrostatic mike. A small, but powerful omni-directional **microphone**.

cone (*VT*, *film*) for soft, gentle lighting effects – a cone-shaped light.

conference organiser (*BT*) someone who organises the administration of a conference. This person is more usually encountered when the conference is organised as a self-financing, hopefully profit-making, venture in its own right, as opposed to the in-company variety. Conference organisers promote the event, sell tickets and deal with all the activities like invitations, catering and so on, but normally turn to a **conference producer** to handle equipment, **software** and the **all-singing, all-dancing** bit. In business theatre, suitably qualified employees at the conference production company will usually handle the organisation as well as the production.

conference producer (*BT*) takes care of everything that actually concerns the sight and sound within a conference. In a smaller production company the producer will sometimes act as **conference organiser** as well. But, more often than not, the producer has his or her hands full with arranging slide–tape, **multi-image modules**, any film or videotape to be shown, plus hiring, setting up and running all the **hardware** needed for sound and pictures. The producer will also organise actors, dancers, musicians and every other component part of the presentation. Often the producer will act as **director** as well, running all on-stage performances, coaching speakers, etc.

continental seating (*BT*) the way seats are laid out at a **venue**, with no central aisle but with plenty of space between rows for audience members to move about.

continuity (*VT, film*) although some people wouldn't agree with me, continuity is the logic of a production. Strictly speaking, it means the painstaking record of every detail of every scene shot in a programme or film, so that when it is edited you don't have **props** appearing to have moved or people transporting themselves thousands of miles in a split second. Needless to say, most productions are shot in anything but the right order – hence the need for careful continuity. The reasons for shooting in the wrong order are wide and varied, but usually boil down to cost and logic. Continuity makes sure the production ends up in the right order and that the whole thing flows in a logical fashion.

70

control track (*VT*) a signal which is recorded on to a video-tape. This tells the **playback** machine what to do during replay.

copy (*VT, film, ST, sound*) a copy, as the word suggests, is a copy of the main **master** copy. In videotape, film, and sound production, **playback** copies will often be on a smaller, lower-quality medium than that of the master. With slide–tape, however, copies will merely be **duped** off the master.

C

corpse (*BT*) for one performer to 'corpse' another is to make the other laugh, thereby injecting a normally unwanted bit of comedy into a script. Usually the laughter can be suppressed, but often the second performer's next line is either confused or forgotten.

crab (*VT, film*) remember how a crab moves? Sideways. To instruct a camera to crab left or right means that it should move, without turning, to whichever side is indicated.

crane (*VT*) a very large camera mounting with wheels. This gives the camera the greatest possible manoeuvrability inside a studio.

crane shot (*VT*) a shot taken by a camera mounted on a **crane**.

crash zoom (*VT, film*) as the name suggests, a very fast **zoom** in to a **shot**.

credits (*VT, film, ST*) the little written back-pats given to contributors at the end of a **production**. Unlike the feature film business, there aren't normally twenty minutes of credits at the end of a show, listing everyone including the tea lady. However, a few discreet **captions** crediting writer, **director**, **producer**, **production company** and **facilities company** is considered a fair courtesy by most clients.

creep (*VT*) any slight gradual failing of electronic equipment, falling away from its normally perfect condition. Also referred to as **drift**, but considered slightly less serious.

creepie-peepie (*VT*) a small VT camera that's hand-held.

Often used by TV crews for close-up shots of sports, crowd scenes, etc.

crew (*VT*, *film*, *BT*) the people who work on a **production**. This does *not* include actors or other performers. It will sometimes be qualified, e.g. camera crew, **stage crew**, **production crew**, **rigging crew**, **technical crew**.

crispener (*VT*) a control used in the VT studio in order to increase the horizontal resolution on screen.

cross colour (*VT*) the problem of colour throbbing on screen, usually on a small area like someone's clothing. Often the problem will be associated with red, which might be fluttering.

cross fade (*VT*, *ST*) to **fade up** one image, while fading down the previous one. Needs a minimum of two slide projectors, or can be done in a videotape edit suite.

cross talk (*VT*, *sound*, *ST*) unexpected breakthrough between parallel channels of a programme chain. Also happens with the **soundtracks** of slide–tape programmes, with one channel playing back a bit from the next-door track. With slide–tape, if there is cross talk between a soundtrack and a **programming** track, the end result is a screeching noise.

crowsfoot (*VT*, *film*) a floor base for a light; has three legs.

crushing (*VT*) when a telephoto lens is used, the end result on screen looks very foreshortened. This is known as crushing.

CSO (*VT*) stands for colour separation overlay. Known in America – and Europe, too, these days – as Chromakey. If you recall television news programmes, you may remember seeing a presenter who appears to be sitting in front of a full screen of changing pictures. This effect is created by the colour separation overlay technique. Through an electronic device, the background colour, usually blue, will be replaced by whatever picture is required. The studio foreground will stay as it is – provided there is no blue on it anywhere, as that could pick up the picture. This is also the technique used in fancy effects on videotape, where you'll see, for example, someone 'walking' on top of a mushroom. Clever stuff.

CU (*VT*, *film*, *ST*) stands for close up.
See also **shot lengths**

cue (*all*) a word you'll hear a lot in this business. Its meanings vary slightly from one medium to another, but one umbrella definition for all is: a cue is a signal, either verbal, written or gesticulated, that indicates a time or place when something new should happen. Used as a verb, to cue means to provide that signal. Let's clarify this with a few examples. (1) In business theatre a slide cue is a written symbol on a speaker's **script**, a copy of which the **programmer** will follow while the person is speaking. At each place within the script where one of these symbols crops up, the programmer will put up the next slide or slides. (2) The size of a slide–tape programme is often determined by its number of cues, i.e. slide changes. In a **multi-image** programme, the number of cues can run into thousands. (3) Actors will take their 'cue' to come on stage, exit, stand on their heads, or whatever, from a key word or two said by the actor immediately before them. Great confusion can arise if the previous actor forgets to say that cue line, or changes it – a great source of theatrical jokes. (4) On a sound tape, a cue can be a mark on the tape, made with a **Chinagraph pencil**, to show where a particular item starts.

cue dots (*VT*, *film*) with a videotape programme, the cue dots – usually a white square in one of the top corners of the screen – will show that the programme is over. With film, there will usually be a white circle in the upper right corner; this tells the projectionist that the end of the reel is coming up and warns him or her that a reel change is due.

cue light (*BT*) if a speaker isn't too sure when his or her slide **cues** should occur in the **script**, or if he or she absolutely must **ad lib** a whole speech, the **programmer** can't cue the slides in the normal way. A **panic button** is therefore placed on the **lectern**; pressing this activates a light in the projection area. Each time this cue light comes on the programmer knows that the next slide is needed and activates the projection **rig**. It's not a bad method, provided the slides are in the right order, but there are often slight delays which result in some slides coming up late on screen.

curtains (*BT*) stage curtains. More commonly seen in older **venues** or in theatre. The opening of curtains is often used as part of a stage **reveal** during a conference.

C

cut (*VT, film*)
(1) a videotape or film editing term. It means a simple, no-tricks transition from one shot to the next.
(2) in **scripts** you'll sometimes see the instruction 'cut to . . .' This has the same meaning, i.e. to cut from one scene to the next.
(3) the word a **director** will use when he or she wants the **action** to stop in a hurry. On hearing that word, camera, sound and performers all stop what they're doing.
(4) the verb to cut means to edit a film.

cutaway (*VT, film*) a useful device that creates a refreshing break from the main **action** in a programme or film and allows performers to 'move' from one **location** to another. For example, in a production which consists mainly of a **talking head** describing a product or service, you might use a few cutaway shots of the product or other information for short periods on screen, accompanied just by the **presenter's voice over**. Or if your presenter is talking to camera in New York, you can't just cut to another scene of him doing the same thing in London – you would have a big **continuity** problem. So, between those two shots, you insert a cutaway shot – one of a plane in the air is probably a bit corny, but you'll get the idea.

cut . . . hold (*VT, film*) when a **director** will say if he wants the camera to stop running temporarily. The 'hold' part means that all performers should hold their positions, rather than wander off, while adjustments are made to lighting, camera positions, etc. Usually **shooting** starts again pretty quickly.

cutter (*film*) a more informal term for a film **editor**.

cutting copy (*film*) the first positive print of a film. This is the one that gets hacked about by the **editor**.

cutting room (*film*) a term meaning the **editing** room; the place where cutting of the film is done. Hence cutting room floor, where many indifferent sequences of film end their days!

cyclorama (*BT*) a **backcloth** that stretches round the back of a stage. Sometimes it's curved. Also abbreviated to cyc.

C

D

dailies (*film*) the first, and completely unedited, prints of the day's work in filming. These are usually looked at, warts and all, the same evening or next morning. Also known as rushes.

dancing boys (*BT*) usually accompany **dancing girls** in really big **productions**. A useful addition to balance the diplomatic score where there is a significant female contingent in the audience.

dancing girls (*BT*) sometimes considered a useful commodity to inspire the sort of hard-nut male audiences you find in the motor trade and other similar industries. An expensive way of creating a mood because with the dancing girls usually go a choreographer, specially composed and recorded music, etc. More popular in America, where high-camp show business creeps into most business theatre.

day for night (*film*) a technique whereby you can put special filters over the camera lens and make broad daylight look more or less like night time. The reason for doing this is to save money; crews charge a hefty amount of overtime to work unsocial hours, so the more **shooting** you can do during the day, the more comfortable for the **budget**.

DBS (*VT*) stands for direct broadcasting by satellite. More a term you'll hear in **broadcast** television, but increasingly popular now for high-budget **teleconference** work.

DBX (*sound*) a trade name for a system which reduces all unwanted extra noise you get from sound recording equipment on the **master** tape.

deaf aid (*VT, BT*) a rather rude nickname for the tiny earpiece worn by **presenters**. The device is in fact a small radio receiver, down which the **director** or **producer** gives instructions to the person concerned. Only necessary when the programme is live, or in **teleconferencing** and business theatre.

de-bag (*VT, film*) a way of camouflaging baggy eyes from the all-seeing eye of the camera. Done by the use of make-up.

definition (*ST, VT, film, sound*) the degree of fine detail either visible in a picture or audible in a sound tape.

demo (*sound*) abbreviation for demonstration tape. Usually used as a halfway step when music is being composed for a **show**. The music is recorded very cheaply, with the minimum number of performers and instruments, just to give the client a feel of what it will ultimately sound like. If approval is given, then a full recording can be done with less chance of the client hating it at the end of the day. The technique can also extend to recordings of **narrations** as well.

demonstration (*VT, film, ST, BT*) one of the greatest advantages of all audio-visual media – the opportunity to *show* your audience or viewers what you're telling them about. Long theoretical explanations about a product, service or technique belong in textbooks and brochures. Demonstration, with the vision complemented by the sound, is by far the best way to educate and motivate. Good demonstration means showing the audience or viewer as much as possible of the topic concerned. Long lectures from a speaker or presenter, with little or no other visual material, defeats the object of the exercise. Audiences and viewers have eyes as well as ears, and anyone who produces programmes and films in this business should rate both ears *and* eyes as equally important recipients of a client's message.

depress (*VT, film*) a camera instruction. It means to lower the camera vertically. Opposite of **elevate**.

depth of field (*VT, film, ST*) the space away from a camera lens within which everything can be seen more or less in focus.

depth of focus (*VT*, *film*, *ST*) the distance beyond a camera lens within which subjects can be moved without the need to re-focus.

desert dolly (*VT*, *film*) a platform on wheels, used to transport big lights around within a **VT** **studio** or sound **stage**.

desk (*BT*, *VT*, *sound*) a control panel. In business theatre it will be the control area that handles sound, lighting and some-times projection **cues**. In a videotape **editing suite** it's the panel from which the **editor** activates all the machinery. In a sound studio the meaning is much the same, but from a sound desk you control not only the editing but the actual sound recording too.

desk-top unit (*ST*) any self-contained unit which will project slides and play back the synchronised **sound track**, all in a format that can be easily carried around and set up in some-one's office. An example of this is the **Caramate**. Some look like TV sets, **back projecting** the slides from within. Others **front project** on to a portable screen which can be set up a few feet away.

dialogue (*all*) scripted spoken speech which is performed as live **action** by actors or other performers. This is as opposed to **commentary**, which is unscripted and **ad-lib**bed, either **to camera** or out of vision, and **narration**, which is usually scripted and spoken out of vision.

digital effects (*VT*) an umbrella term for all the fancy **computer-generated** effects you can achieve with a well-equipped videotape **editing suite**.

dip (*VT*) a metal cover on the floor of the studio that prevents people from tripping over the electrical sockets immediately beneath.

directional mike (*sound*) a **microphone** which is particularly sensitive to sounds coming from one direction.
    See also **directivity, omni-directional mike, rifle mike**

directivity (*sound*) noun from directional. Used in connection with microphones.
See also **directional mike, omni-directional mike**

director (*VT*, *film*, *BT*)
(1) in the case of videotape and film, the director is the person who directs the creative aspects of both the performers and the camera crew. He or she also officiates at the **edit** stage, working hand in hand with the VT or film **editor**, and will make final decisions on **casting**, too.
(2) in business theatre the director will usually just be concerned with directing on-stage performances; the **producer** runs the **crew**. In fact, in all but the largest of **shows**, the producer performs both functions.

disc (*sound*, *VT*) *see* **disk**

disk (*sound*, *VT*) in the sound studio, a disk (or disc) is merely a record, as we know it. In video terms, however, the picture gets more complicated.
See also **video disk**

dissolve (*ST*, *VT*, *film*) a technique whereby one picture **fades down** slowly as the next picture **fades up**. Very like the **cross-fade** technique. With slide you need two **projectors** to do it, with videotape a properly equipped **editing suite**. With film, the dissolve is done in the laboratory, not the **cutting room**.
See also **mix**

dissolve unit (*ST*) a machine which instructs two or more projectors to **dissolve** from one slide to the next, either by a manual **cue** or from a tape-cue **pulse**.

dobson (*VT*, *film*) usually, the last rehearsal of a **shot** before the camera begins to **roll**.

dock (*BT*) the part of a theatre or **venue** where equipment and scenery can be offloaded and stored. Also known, more traditionally, as scene-dock.

docudrama (*VT*, *film*) *see* **dramadoc**

documentary (*ST, VT, film*) a straightforward factual representation of a story or message; a script style that comes over in the un-fussy way of a news broadcast or television documentary.

Dolby (*sound*) a trade name for a system which, on the **master** tape, reduces all the unwanted extra noise you get from sound recording equipment.

dolly (*VT, film*)
(1) A wheeled mounting of any kind on which a camera can be mounted.
(2) To dolly means to move the camera around on its dolly.

domino (*BT*) a lighting source that lights up the **cyclorama** and back area of the stage.

dope sheet (*VT, film*) *see* **camera script**

double exposure (*film, ST*) the act of exposing one **frame** of film twice so that you get a combination of two images on one slide. This is done at photographic stage.

double head (*film*) the way in which a film can be viewed with its accompanying **soundtrack** during the **editing** process. Vision is on one piece of film, sound on another, and the two are projected together – hence the term.

double track (*sound*) a technique whereby one singer (or musician) can get two sounds, almost for the price of one. However cynics say that double tracking is a useful device to cover up a less than wonderful voice quality. The singer (and it is more usually a singer, although the technique can in theory be used for any single sound) sings his or her part, which is recorded. It is then played back to the singer through the **cans** as a **guide track**, and he or she sings along with it. The second voice track is then **mix**ed in with the first. As there will be an inevitable fractional delay between the first and second voices, you get a fuller, more interesting, double-track effect.

downstage (*BT*) *see* **stage directions**

dramadoc (*VT, film, ST*) also known as a docudrama. In effect, the halfway house between a **documentary** and a **dramatisation**. It is the re-enactment, by actors or models, of an actual event which has occurred in real life. The term can also be used to describe **faction**.

dramatisation (*ST, VT, film*) the enacting of a fictitious story or message, using actors or models. In this business, a typical dramatisation might occur in a safety training film, where actors portray what can happen in an office or factory if fire breaks out; or in sales training, where actors demonstrate the 'right' and 'wrong' selling techniques to a 'customer'.

D

drapes (*BT, VT*) all soft fabrics, hanging or otherwise, that are used on stage or in a studio.

dress (*VT, film, BT*)
(1) to get a **set** prepared for shooting or, in the case of business theatre, for final **rehearsal**. This means all **props** and other equipment must be in place.
(2) an abbreviation for **dress rehearsal**.

dresser (*BT*) someone backstage who helps performers in and out of their costumes. Made famous by a British film of the same name.

dress rehearsal (*BT*) in theatrical terms, a dress rehearsal means a full **rehearsal** of a play, with all performers in costume. In business theatre, especially when all performers are speakers rather than actors, you don't normally bother to put the speakers in their best suits! However, it does mean that the whole **show** is rehearsed, including any **modules** and videotape or film **inserts**, in correct order. Any actors or models involved *will* be in costume. The dress rehearsal is usually the last before the show, or before the first show of a **roadshow**.
See also **technical rehearsal, top and tail rehearsal**

drift (*VT*) when the efficacity of a camera is on the slippery downward slope. A more serious problem than **creep**.

81

drop in (*ST, BT*)
(1) any bit of **graphics** which is superimposed on to an existing photograph, either during film **processing** or in a **montage**.
(2) when you're **programming** a **show**, any slides which are late will usually be called drop-ins. That's because for programming purposes you use a **write-on** slide and drop the final slide in when it's ready.

dropout (*sound, VT*)
(1) a fleeting stop or gap in a signal from an audio tape, usually caused by a small imperfection.
(2) little white sparkling bits that appear on screen, caused by impurities in the oxide coating of an inferior bit of videotape.

drop shadow (*ST, VT, film*) a shadow down one or two sides of an object – usually lettering – to emphasise it in relief. Can be done by hand at **artwork** stage, or it can be **computer generated**.

dry (*BT*) to dry up, to forget your lines or lose your thread when **ad lib**bing. A word pinched from traditional theatre.

dry hire (*all*) an expression used to show that equipment hired comes just as it stands; the hire does not include **crew** or operators for it, and the hirer must operate it him or herself. Opposite of **wet hire**.

dry ice fog (*BT, VT, film*) creates a misty, foggy effect at low level either live in business theatre, or in a studio for videotape or film. Consists of solid carbon dioxide either dunked in hot water or with steam blown over it. Most performers complain of very cold ankles when working with dry ice fog, but the dramatic effect can be spectacular, particularly if you play coloured lights through the mists.

dub (*VT, film, sound*) *see* **dubbing**

dubbing (*VT, film, sound*)
(1) to assemble all pre-recorded material for a programme or film and re-record it into one harmonious **mix**.
(2) sometimes, too, actors will dub their own voices on to a

soundtrack for a film; very often the sound quality recorded on **location** is poor, so to do it over again in a studio gives far better results.

(3) professional singers will dub their voices over an actor's on film where the actors appear to be singing, in lip sync.

(4) foreign languages can be dubbed on to a film in another language.

dupe (*ST, film*) abbreviation of duplicate or duplication. Whether you're talking about slides or films, it's important to remember that dupes must always be taken from the original **master**. Dupes taken from dupes will never be as good in quality; the more **generations** a slide or film goes through in copying, the worse the quality gets.

Dutchman (*BT*)
(1) a fabric strip which you can use to conceal the joins in theatrical **sets** or **flats**.
(2) the rigid supports used to hold scenery up.

Dutch tilt (*VT, film*) to turn a camera to an unusual angle, i.e. not on the horizontal. Can produce quite interesting effects.

DVE (*VT*) stands for digital video effects.
See also **digital effects**

E

edge numbers (*film*, *ST*) numbers actually processed into the edge of a film or, in the case of slides, along the edge of each exposure on a 35 mm roll. These help to identify which bits are where. Useful when editing.

edit (*VT*, *film*, *sound*) used as a noun to describe each individual function required in the editing process, more usually in videotape production, e.g. 'That was a complicated programme – over a hundred edits and only ten minutes long.'
  See also **editing**

editing (*all*) editing in this business means much the same as it would in a newspaper office. You always generate more initial creative material – be it sound recording, videotape, film or slides – than you need (far better to have too much than too little). Then you have to edit that down to the final programme or film length. The individual processes vary, of course. Videotape editing is done electronically, essentially re-recording the necessary bits from the initial tapes on to one **master** tape. Film and sound tapes are both edited by physically cutting out what you don't want. Slides are edited by simply discarding those which are superfluous.

editing suite (*VT*) the rooms in which videotape editing is done. With all the electronic and computerised equipment used nowadays, even small editing suites can look like the main control room in *Star Trek*. But don't be baffled by science; what you can expect to see is a selection of TV screens on the wall in front of you – these are called **monitors**. Naturally, the numbers and placings will vary from suite to suite, but in the main you'll see some small black and white screens on which you can look through and call up each of your original tapes. Then there'll be two larger, colour screens: one, usually on the

84

left, will be the preview or rehearse monitor on which you preview the **edit** in question; the other large colour screen will show you what you have on your **master** tape. Other machinery will include the main control panel, plus perhaps such machinery as **caption** generators, and other **special effects** devices. The machines that actually play all the tapes will be in another room – certainly in the case of **1-inch** editing suites and above. The **editor** will talk to the people in their other rooms over a **microphone** link.

editor (*VT, film*) the person who operates the machinery to edit videotape or film. Good editors are very skilled people and are some of the most highly esteemed – and well paid – experts in the business.

E

edit pulse (*VT*) an edit pulse is a magnetic signal on the control track of a videotape recording. It tells you where one sequence of pictures finishes and, again, when the next begins.

effects (*or* **special effects**) (*all*) anything which is not part of the mainstream **live-action** subject-matter of taping, filming, recording, etc. Special effects on film include such space battle scenes as in *Star Wars*. Videotape effects, often called **digital effects**, are used to move pictures around and create fancy scenes such as you might see in a rock music video. Theatrical special effects can include **dry ice fog**, **smoke machines**, etc. Slide–tape effects will include elaborate **graphics** sequences, complicated **build-ups** and so on. And **sound effects** are any pre-recorded sound you add on to the main subject, like a ringing doorbell or street noises.

EFP (*VT*) stands for electronic field production. Normally pertains to television, where a large crew using several cameras are employed on location for a specific event, e.g. a sports match. This can either be broadcast live or can be taped for transmission or showing later.

egg crate (*VT, film*) a piece of equipment put in front of a light to stop the diffused beam going beyond that point.

8 mm (*film*) film that is 8 mm wide; the smallest and most basic type. Used in the past by amateurs – the original home movies medium.

See also **70 mm, 16 mm, super 8 mm, 35 mm**

EJ (*VT*) stands for electronic journalism. Refers to the sort of news reporting you get with lightweight portable cameras and a very small **crew**.

See also **ENG**

Ektographic (*ST*) a trade name (Kodak) for a clear, plain slide upon which you can write whatever you want.

See also **write ons**

elevate (*VT, film*) a camera instruction. It means to raise the camera vertically.

See also **depress**

ELS (*VT, film, ST*) stands for extremely long shot.

See also **shot lengths**

encoding (*ST, BT*) the act of placing electronic pulses on the **master** sound tape of a **slide–tape** programme. These pulses direct the projectors, through suitable intermediary equipment.

ENG (*VT*) stands for electronic news gathering. Usually pertains to television, where a small **crew** with just one portable camera covers an event.

engineer (*sound*) more or less self-explanatory – the person who operates the machinery in a sound studio during both recording and **mixing**. Not necessarily the same person who carries out the repairs, though.

English (*VT, film*) a lighting term, describing the way **barn doors** are placed over a light to create vertical slits.

establishing shot (*VT, film*) an expression used in **scripts**. Establishing shots are mood setters, really; usually short general background shots to show a certain amount of information about the action which follows, e.g. the outside of a building inside which the next **scene** takes place, or a panoramic view of a city where the story is set.

explosion wipe (*VT*) a gimmicky way of changing from one picture to the next. The new picture bursts quite rapidly from the centre of the screen, spreading quickly over the whole area and replacing the previous picture.

ext (*ST, VT, film*) abbreviation for **exterior**.

exterior (*ST, VT, film*) any photography, videotaping or filming which has to be done in the open air. More usually seen on **scripts** where such a **shot** or **scene** is required. Sometimes abbreviated to ext.

E

extra (*VT, film*) second-division actors on a production. They don't have speaking parts, other than that of background conversation or 'rhubarb rhubarb' noise-making roles. Used for crowd scenes, street scenes, filling up a restaurant or hotel lobby **interior shot**, etc.

eyeline (*VT, film*) the line of eye contact between a performer and the camera or between two performers – in the latter case a tricky one from the **continuity** point of view. If you're **shooting** a **scene** with two or more performers from several different angles (for a more interesting edited result) you must be careful that the logic of their eyelines is right on each different camera angle, otherwise, in the finished production, you can get the impression that the performers are staring about wildly in several different directions.

F

facilities house (*ST, VT, film*) a company which offers all the facilities required to make a programme or film except for the functions of producing, directing, writing, etc. Normally, smaller **production companies** don't have all their own facilities such as costumes, cameras, **editing suites**, slide-making equipment and so on. So, when such a production company has been hired by a client, it will in turn hire a facilities house to provide all the back-up and production services required. Sometimes people who run facilities houses try to get in on the **production** side as well, going after business in the client sector, in competition with production companies. This is sometimes unwise, though; a facilities house doing some production as well will pose a risk – real or imagined – to any production companies taking their own clients there.

faction (*VT, film*) the **script** and performing style used to portray a largely fictional story in a **documentary** manner.
See also **dramadoc**

fade in/out (*all*) *see* **fade up/down**

fader (*VT, sound*) any lever or control which is used manually to **fade up** or **fade down** a picture or sound.

fade up/down (*all*) a gradual, rather than abrupt, beginning or ending. In visual terms it means to bring a picture up from, or fade it down to, black. In sound terms it simply means a gradual increase or decrease in volume, from silence to full **level** or vice versa. Fade in/out means exactly the same thing.

feed (*VT, BT*)
(1) in videotape, feed is just a nickname for the process of

transmitting a signal either from one machine to another or (in TV) broadcasting or transmitting a programme.

(2) in theatre, however, a feed is a performer who 'feeds' straight statements to a comic.

feedback (*BT*, *sound*) more correctly, acoustic feedback. Gives an ear-splitting screech when a **microphone** picks up its own amplified signal from a **speaker**. Instant cure is to lower the volume. A good precaution against it happening is to make sure the microphone is behind the speakers and that the speakers are not facing towards the microphone.

field (*VT*) half of a videotape picture. Each **frame** in videotape consists of two intertwined fields, of 312.5 lines each on **PAL** and **SECAM** systems and 262.5 on an **NTSC** system.

film horse (*film*) a contraption used in film editing to separate out various sections of film.

film recording (*VT/film*) a process whereby you transfer a videotape production on to film. The opposite, if you like, of **telecine**.

film storyboard (*film*, *VT*) a way of demonstrating how a finished production – usually a commercial – will look without going to all the expense and trouble of making it first. Elements from the drawn **storyboard** are rostrum-filmed in sequence, and sometimes a **demo soundtrack** is produced to go with it. This can then be shown to the client for approval, before going on to the final production. Film storyboards have now been largely replaced by **animatics**, which are the videotaped equivalents. Animatics cost less because you don't have any processing costs and editing is minimised.

filmstrip (*film/ST*) a sort of halfway house between slides and motion pictures. Individual slides are reproduced on 35 mm film and the filmstrip is then projected one **frame** at a time along with a pre-recorded **soundtrack**. In theory, this method is lighter and easier to carry around than a **magazine** of slides but, like many compromises, it has its problems and is not very popular these days. Although it once was a reasonable method of transferring a slide–tape programme to a somewhat more convenient medium, it is now being replaced by the infinitely better videotape transfer.

film tree (*film*) a wooden device seen in cutting rooms that holds various **clips** of edited film ready for **splicing** together.

filter (*ST, film*) a gelatin or glass square or disc, appropriately coloured to create specific effects. It's put right over the camera lens, altering the colour and quality of light that gets on to the finished product. Coloured filters can be very useful in correcting less-than-ideal light conditions. And filters with special effects, like the **star filter**, can create a very interesting mood for a **shot**.

final cut (*film*) the last product of the film **editing** process, and effectively the last opportunity for the **production** team to change anything before the **show copy** is made.

F

fine cut (*VT*) the videotape equivalent of the film business's **final cut** – the last stage in editing before the **show copy** or transmission copy is sent out.

fine-grain print (*film*) a higher-than-normal quality of film, with no silver salt deposits which cause eventual deterioration. Used to produce duplicate negatives.

Finsbury (*VT, film*) a purely British term, from cockney rhyming slang. Finsbury Park = arc, as in **arc** light.

firing step (*BT*) a small platform in the **flies** area above the stage, where ropes and other lightweight equipment can be stored out of sight.

fish-eye lens (*VT, film, ST*) a camera lens which, on the final image, gives the impression that it has been **shot** from the bottom of a goldfish bowl. The effect looks like a convex mirror, arising from the fact that a fish-eye is about the widest angle of lens you can get – 160°.

fishpole (*VT, film*) a microphone **boom**, about 6–7 feet long, held by an operator.

fit-up (*BT*) a temporary **set**, including a stage or performing area, that can be taken down and put up again in several **venues**. Used for **roadshows**, where the same **show** is being done in a number of locations on a tour.

fixer (*sound*) a term you're most likely to hear when music has to be recorded. A fixer will hire musicians and singers according to availability and suitability, and if necessary will hire a recording **studio** as well.

flag (*VT*, *film*) a large square board which you can use either to shade the camera itself or to block off part of a light's beam.

flash (*ST*) a programming/projection term. The **show** is **programmed** so that at a given time, with a particular slide in a **projector**, the projector light will flash on and off a pre-specified number of times.

flat (*BT*, *film*, *VT*) any flat piece of scenery. Predominantly taken to mean the flat boards or panels used in business theatre to make up the stage **set**. There are many different types of flat used in this business, and they are classified in this book under their individual names.

flicker (*ST*) a programming/projection term. The **show** is **programmed** so that at a given time, with a particular slide in a **projector**, the projector light will flicker for a pre-specified length of time.

flies (*BT*) the area where the ropes and pulley systems operate to **fly** scenery or equipment on stage.

flip chart (*BT*) the first and most elementary stage of audio-visual communications – an easel with a pad of paper on it, hinged at the top so the speaker can draw or write on a sheet, flip it over and start again. Useless for all but the smallest of audiences, and not too effective unless the speaker's pretty good at drawing and talking at the same time.

flood (*VT*, *film*, *BT*) any light source which is general rather than focused on a particular object.

floodlight (*VT, film, BT*) *see* **flood**

floor manager (*VT, film*) the person who, when taping or filming is being done in a **studio**, organises all movement of equipment, **props**, etc. He or she also passes messages on to the performers from the **director**; this is done through a **headset** which allows two-way communication between the floor manager and the control area, where the director sits. You'll find many more floor managers in VT than in film, as filming tends to take place with everyone – director included – in one place.

flop (*ST*) to turn a slide over on the horizontal plane. Sometimes handy to create special mirror-image effects. Sometimes done accidentally, when it's hard to tell – unless there are words on the slide, of course.

flutter (*sound*)
(1) a very fast fluctuation in volume or pitch of a sound.
(2) variation in recording speed quicker than a fifteenth of a second.

fly (*BT*) to fly scenery or equipment on stage you raise or lower it with ropes and pulley systems operated above the stage.

fly on the wall (*VT, film*) a camera production approach, usually used in **documentary** productions. The camera becomes an eavesdropper, in effect; recording a natural unrehearsed conversation or meeting, with no-one speaking directly **to camera** and no **narration** to describe what's going on. It allows the viewer to feel that he or she is actually present during that meeting, albeit without a speaking part, through the eye of the camera lens.

focal length (*VT, film, ST*) the distance between the main object of focus and the optical middle of the lens itself.

focus (*BT*) the main **spotlight**, usually used to light the main performer.

focus puller (*VT, film*) an assistant to the cameraman. He or

F

92

she is responsible for the fine tuning of lens focus while taping or filming is being done. May also **load** tape or films as well.

fold back (*sound*) a recording **studio** term. When a **voice over**, or anyone else for that matter, is speaking into a **microphone**, he or she will be sitting in an extremely well-sound-proofed **box**, as will a singer in a music **session**. In such an environment the person's voice doesn't sound normal, which is annoying for the talker and very off-putting for the singer. People in the box therefore have the choice of wearing **cans** through which they can hear their own voice, in exactly the same way that the equipment is recording it. The term fold back comes from the fact that the person's voice is going from his or her own mouth, down the **microphone**, through to the equipment and back down to the person again via the cans. An advantage of fold back is that the **engineer** can control the volume to suit each person's own ears.

F

follow spot (*VT*, *film*, *BT*) a **spotlight** on a pivot, usually operated by hand, that follows a performer in the **studio** or on **stage**.

footage (*film*) the length of a film, worked out in feet. Used mainly as a loose term to describe sections of film, e.g. 'We need to **shoot** some more footage of the exterior of the building' or 'Please call the so-and-so film library and ask if they have any footage of one-legged pelicans,' etc.

footlight (*BT*) in traditional theatre, one of the lights placed in the **downstage** edge of the stage, pointing towards the performers – at their feet, so to speak.

Forox (*ST*) a brand name for a type of **rostrum camera**.

four waller (*VT*, *film*) a completely enclosed **set** with adjustable walls. The camera can move about freely inside the 'walls'.

FPS (*film*)
(1)   stands for feet per second.
(2)   stands for **frames** per second.

frame (*ST, film*) with slides, one frame is one exposure on a roll of film. The film is then cut up, frame by frame, and those to be used are mounted up as slides. With film, the principle is the same, except, of course, that the film moves through a **projector** at the usual speed of twenty-four frames per second. The word is also used to describe the stationary television image.

frame jog capability (*VT*) when passing videotape through on **playback** when **editing**, frame jog capability means you can stop the tape anywhere you like on any given image. With film editing, of course, it's much easier as each frame is a nice convenient oblong shape. With VT, though, the magnetic recording technique means that you don't get a symmetrical frame shape. Frame jog capability, then, is a somewhat complicated attribute.

F

freelance (*all*) freelance means to be self-employed, working on your own. Many people in this business are freelance, especially **scriptwriters**, choreographers and **directors**. A few **producers** are freelance, but most work as employees or principals of **production companies**. On the technical side, quite a few **programmers** and sound **engineers** are also freelance. Some clients and some production companies get a bit nervous about there being a number of freelance people on a **crew** – they feel that for security and continuity reasons everyone should be a member of a production company's staff. What they forget is that, quite apart from the obvious financial good sense of hiring freelance people only when you need them, you can pick the best in the business for a given job. And if anyone is worried about loyalty and security, they can forget that too; a freelance person would only manage to leak confidential information, or be disloyal to his or her clients, once. The business is still small, even in the US; word gets around so fast that the disloyal freelancer would never work again. The truth is that if you're making a good living as a freelance, you're bound to be good at your job – so, from the client's point of view, hiring a busy successful freelancer is a reasonable guarantee of quality.

freeze frame (*film, VT*) when a single **frame** is held so that all motion on screen appears to stop. With videotape it's likely to be done just by stopping the tape. With film, several identical frames will be printed into the film so that, although the image will appear static, the film will still be moving through the **projector** at normal speed.

front axial projection (*VT, film*) a process which involves projecting a background scene, via the axis of a camera lens, on to a glass beaded screen which is very reflective.

front projection (*VT, film, ST*) projecting from the audience's side of the **screen** as opposed to **back projection**. Front projection is well suited to small **venues** as the screen can be flush with a wall, leaving plenty of space for the audience between that and the **projector** at the back of the room.

frost (*VT, film, BT*) a filter that diffuses light.

F stop (*ST, film*) *see* **stop**

fuff (*VT, film, BT*) phoney snow, used to create wintery effects.

FX (*all*) stands for 'effects'.
    See also **SFX**

F

G

gaffer (*VT*, *film*, *BT*) the most senior electrician on the **crew**.

gaffer tape (*VT*, *film*, *BT*) heavy-duty electrical insulating tape, about 2 inches wide. In theory, part of the **gaffer**'s domain but in practice one of the most highly praised bits of equipment in the business. Many's the problem that can be solved with good old gaffer tape, particularly in business theatre. Gaffer tape sticks wires and cables down to carpets, walls, etc., so audiences and crew don't trip over them, and white gaffer tape stuck on the bases of light stands and other protruding ironmongery prevents untold bruised shins and embarrassing crashes in darkened conference **venues**.

gag (*all*) any joke which is introduced into a **script**, rather than one which arises naturally out of the subject matter concerned.

gallery (*VT*) in large videotape **studios** the gallery is the main control room located above and overlooking the main studio floor beneath. **Production crew** in the gallery look on through soundproofed windows and communicate over the **talk-back** system.

gate (*film*, *ST*) the part of the **projector** or camera through which the film travels at the time of projection on screen or of photography. Also applies to a slide being projected.

gel (*ST*) abbreviation for gelatin, although in fact it means sections of translucent colour film. In slide–tape production a coloured gel can be inserted into a slide mount behind, say, a **lith** word or other **graphics**. Lith, projected on its own, comes out as white lettering, etc.; with the gel it will project as whatever colour the gel consists of.

generation (*ST*, *VT*, *film*, *sound*) the stages of copying a recording, programme or film beyond the **master**. For example, a **VHS** copy of a videotape programme, copied from a **U-matic** version which has been taken from a **1-inch** master, would be third generation. If you copied some more VHS tapes from your original VHS, they would be fourth generation. And the quality would be lousy, too – the more generations, the worse it gets.

generator (*VT*, *film*, *BT*) *see* **genny**

genny (*VT*, *film*, *BT*) abbreviation for the portable electricity generator used to power lights and other equipment on **location** or at a **venue**. Usually gennies are mounted on a truck and are driven by diesel motors, which can create sound problems.

get in/out (*BT*) the occasion and procedure of getting all presentation equipment in and out of the **venue**. Sometimes includes to **rig** and de-rig, plus building and **striking** the **set**. This can involve as little as a couple of well-muscled men and a van or as much as a whole theatrical **crew** including **chippies**, **sparks**, a dozen more able-bodied individuals, a twitching **set designer** with an armful of plans and a **producer** trying to set the whole thing to music. Strictly speaking, in theatrical terms, the get-in means physically getting the equipment in, and that's it, but in business theatre it overspills as there's seldom time for get-in and rigging to run consecutively. The get-in is usually the time-consuming part of the operation, and is especially fraught when there's only a limited amount of time before the **show**. This explains why clients often see red eyes in unshaven faces among conference crews, for whom one, two or even three all-night stints are just part of the job. Get-outs don't take as long because by this time everybody knows which bits go where and which cases should contain what equipment.

ghost (*VT*, *film*, *ST*) with videotape and film, this is a faint secondary image which appears adjacent to the main one. The videotape problem is caused by a mistiming of the signal; the film version is usually a hiccup in projection. With slide–tape, ghosting will happen when a **projector** doesn't dim properly or when there's a design fault in the optical equipment.

ghost crew (*VT*, *film*) if you take a camera crew abroad, the trade unions in some countries will insist that you hire a complementary local crew, even if they sit around all day while your own crew does the work. This local group is called a ghost crew.

glass shot (*film*) a shot that cheats. Part of the scenery in the foreground, rather than being specially built, is painted on glass in suitable proportions. The camera shoots through the glass and picks up the performers, plus all the genuine background scenery, beyond. Saves a lot of money and elaborate **sets**.

glitch (*all*) an across-the-board word for a small hiccup or fault, used throughout the technological jargon of the world (especially that of computers). Has crept into this business since much of the equipment used today is computerised. Comes from Yiddish, to slide.

G

go (*BT*) an instruction given by whoever is calling a **show** over the **cans**, telling the operators of the various equipment when to start, e.g. '**Stand by houselights**; stand by **walk-out music**. **Kill lectern** mike; kill **screenwash** and stage lights. Go houselights; go walk-out music.'

gobo (*VT*, *film*, *BT*)
(1) a sound-proofed, movable **flat**.
(2) a small black panel which, when put next to a light, creates an interesting lighting effect.

gods (*BT*) a nickname for the highest balcony of seats in traditional theatres.

goes up (*BT*) terminology switched from traditional theatre. A **show** goes up (starts) at a given time.
See also **comes down**

grading (*film*) the way, and action, of ensuring the correct colour balances in prints of a film. This is done by experts in the film laboratory with precisely defined combinations of **filters** and light levels.

grams (*sound*) an old-fashioned word for sound; used to refer to sound recording of films. In the past the **director** of a **shoot** would have instructed 'Roll grams; roll camera; **action!**' Nowadays, though, he or she would just say 'Sound'. The old gramophone, from which grams is abbreviated, has gone the same route as the horseless carriage and the wireless.

graphics (*VT, film, ST*) any part of a **production** which is, or appears to be, drawn rather than photographed.
See also **artwork, computer generated**

green film (*film*) a positive – as opposed to negative – copy of a film, fresh back from the laboratory and probably not even completely dry.

green room (*BT*) a room somewhere near the **backstage** area of a **venue** where crew members and performers can sit, relax and have meals or refreshments while off duty.

grid (*VT, film, BT*) an openwork 'ceiling' above a **studio** or **stage** area, with a walkway for **crew** to move around on. Lights, scenery and so on are hung from the grid.

grind (*VT, film*) slang for projecting or showing a film or programme.

grip (*film*) a **crew** technician who's generally known as a highly-qualified handyman (perhaps it should be handyperson). He or she moves equipment, including the camera **dolly**, and provides assistance whenever it's needed.
See also **key grip**

guide track (*sound, VT*) any **soundtrack** pre-recorded and used to guide a musician or performer while he or she is adding some new sound. The performer will listen to this through the **cans**. Sometimes a guide track will be recorded during the shooting of a programme or film, and used purely as a guide during **post-synchronisation**; a whole new soundtrack will then be recorded in the studio.

GV (*ST, VT, film*) stands for 'general view'; a **script** term. A

GV might be used as an **establishing shot** or to show a general outlook on screen while the **narration** goes over some background points.

G

hair in the gate (*film*) when tiny shavings of emulsion (from the film as it passes through the **gate**) collect like little fibres and get photographed. They must be cleaned out at regular intervals during filming. Sometimes, of course, you can get real hair in the gate of either the camera or a **projector**, especially if the equipment has been sitting around unprotected and there's been a shaggy dog around the studio . . .

halation (*film*) a round halo encircling an image. Usually caused by reflections inside an actual film base.

handbasher (*VT, film*) a light of about 800 watts in power. It's hand-held, hence the name.

hardware (*VT, BT, ST*) all the hard equipment used in production and projection, e.g. cameras, **editing** equipment, **projectors**, etc. As opposed to **software**, which is the tapes, slides and so on. Borrowed from computer terminology.

HDTV (*VT*) stands for high definition television. A Japanese development for a system of TV based on 1,125 lines instead of 525 lines (**NTSC**) or 625 lines (**PAL** and **SECAM**). The **aspect ratio** is also different, at 5 to 3. The HDTV system gives much better quality in picture terms, and it is thought that in time this system will totally replace the poorer 525 and 625 versions in use today. Another advantage of this would be that HDTV would – presumably – permit a standardisation of format all over the world, which would avoid the problems created at the moment by the need to undertake standards conversion from country to country. However at the time of writing HDTV is still at a comparatively early stage in its development and the experts are predicting that we will probably be well into the 1990s before all traces of PAL, SECAM and NTSC have vanished.

head (*VT, sound*) the parts of videotape or audio recording and **playback** equipment that actually touch the tape when it's in motion, so recording or playing back the image or sound.

head clog (*VT*) when the **head** of a videotape recording or **playback** machine gets bunged up with stray particles of oxide lost from the tapes.

head out (*sound*) an audio tape is head out when it has been wound so that you can just **thread** it up and play it, with no need to rewind it first.

headphones (*BT, sound*) *see* **cans**

headset (*VT, film, BT*) a pair of **headphones** with a **microphone** attached which allows two-way communication among all members of the **crew**.

hearing it back (*sound*) listening to whatever has just been recorded, when the tape has been rewound and is played back.

high band (*VT*) a ¾-inch-wide videotape format. It is quite widely used as the master tape for non-broadcast VT programmes as the quality is quite reasonable and the cost of it is low when compared to **1-inch** or **2-inch** videotape. It is officially supposed to be **broadcast-standard** tape; however, very few broadcast programmes are made with it in Europe or the US.
See also **low band, U-matic**

high hat (*VT, film*) a small support used to raise a camera up from ground level.

high speed (*film*) normally film is shot at twenty-four **frames** per second. However, for the effect of **slow motion**, you can shoot the film at a faster rate and then project at the normal speed. High-speed film can be shot at as much as 500 or even 1,000 frames per second. This is used quite a lot in technical or medical films, where very fast movement needs to be analysed carefully. For example, one film used 1,000 frames per second to photograph an athlete running. The camera, which had to be static at that speed, picked up his foot and leg each time he landed on a given place. When the film was processed and projected at normal speed, it showed all the muscle movement that occurs during fast running in ultra-slow motion – something the naked eye could never see and for which videotape slow motion could never have been so effective.

hit (*VT*, *film*, *BT*) to switch something on, e.g. 'Could you hit play button, please?'

honey wagons (*VT*, *film*) a somewhat bizarre euphemism for the portable loos used by **crews** on **location**.

hook (*VT*, *film*, *ST*, *sound*) a major aspect of a **script**, story or piece of music which grabs the audience's attention and/or provides the platform on which to build the whole **production**. For example, the hook of a film on industrial safety might be the **dramatisation** of a typical accident.

hosepiping (*VT*, *film*) a rather rude term to describe bad hand-held camera work, usually by amateurs. The idea is that the operator has held the camera in the same way as someone would while watering the garden with a hosepipe – shakily.

H

hospitality room (*VT*, *film*, *BT*) a room set aside at a **studio**, **editing suite** or business-theatre **venue** where the clients can be entertained, or where clients can entertain their own clients or colleagues. Sometimes euphemistically corrupted into 'hostility room'.

hot (*sound*) written on a piece of paper and stuck, or **China-graphed**, on to a sound-**editing** machine. It indicates that the tape on the machine is being edited and must not be removed for any reason.

hot set (*VT*, *film*, *BT*) a **set** or performing area which has been lit and otherwise prepared for **shooting** or for a **show**.

houselights (*BT*) borrowed from traditional theatre. House-lights are the lights in the audience areas – used while they **walk in**, during any intervals, and when they **walk out**.

house show (*VT*, *film*, *ST*) the presentation a **production company** will give to a prospective client. Will normally contain examples of the company's past work for other clients.

hunting (*VT*, *film*) used to describe a videotape machine or a film camera which can't maintain a steady speed.

hymnbook (*VT*, *film*) the **camera script**.

hyphenate (*all*) when a production **crew** member does two jobs, e.g. **producer-director**, **composer-arranger**, etc.

idiot boards (*VT*, *film*) prompt or **cue** sheets held up beside the camera to remind the performer what to say if there isn't a **teleprompter** available.

idiot box (*VT*, *film*, *BT*) rude nickname for a **teleprompter**.

idiot sheets (*VT*, *film*) *see* **idiot boards**

impractical (*VT*, *film*, *BT*) *see* **unpractical**

in the round (*BT*) a **stage** or performing area which is surrounded by the audience, rather than the conventional theatre format of audience one end, performers the other.

inflection (*sound*) the way a **voice-over** artiste raises and lowers the tone and pitch of the voice in order to convey mood and create interest.

initiation medium (*all*) also called origination medium. Any medium (e.g. videotape, film, etc.) which is used to record or film the original **master** of a production. A programme which is shot on film and then transferred to videotape for showing would be described as having had film as the initiation (or origination) medium, with videotape as the **playback** medium.

insert (*VT*, *film*, *BT*)
(1) in drama, a **shot** which adds background or spice to a main **sequence**.
(2) in business theatre, usually refers to a videotape programme or film which is inserted into the **show**.

insert edit (*VT*) any **edit** which is put in after the main **master** of the programme has been recorded.
   See also **assemble edit**

instrumental track (*sound*) the **soundtracks** in a music recording which contain all the musical instruments concerned. The **vocals**, if required, are normally added on later.

int (*ST, VT, film*) abbreviation for **interior**.

interactive (*VT*) any programme and **playback** system which offers a choice of options to the viewer. Used largely for training, interactive techniques are based on a **monitor** screen, a microcomputer and either a videotape or **video disk** playback system. Typically a programme will set up a proposition, then set some questions for the viewer. Depending on his or her answer, the microcomputer will instruct the tape or disk machine to search for the appropriate next part of the programme, which will then be played back, and so on to the end of the training session.

intercut (*VT, film*) to cut back and forth between two different sequences or camera angles. Creates interest and also helps to build up a sense of tension in drama productions.

interior (*ST, VT, film*) a **script** term. Any **shot** or **scene** which is done indoors.

I

interview (*VT, film, sound*) a very useful way for viewers or listeners to hear information 'from the horse's mouth'. Interviews can be scripted, but these tend to sound stilted. Far better is for the **interviewer** to ask carefully thought-out questions and go through them with the interviewee beforehand so he or she has a chance to figure out what best to say. **Location** interviews can be tricky if there is a lot of **ambient noise**, but they are very realistic, especially if you can show the interviewee actually in his or her place of work. **Studio** interviews are easier to control but can spook the less experienced interviewee.

interviewer (*VT, film, sound*) needs to be a very skilled person in order to put interviewees at ease and ask the sort of questions that will get the best answers. Interviewers can work **on-camera**, which means you see and hear them asking questions, or they can work **off-camera**, which means they're out of vision and you edit out their questions later, leaving just the inter-viewee's responses.

intro (*all*) abbreviation for introduction. Is also used as a verb, e.g. to intro a conference.

ips (*sound*) acronym for inches per second. Measures the speed at which audio tape is recorded and played back. **Reel-to-reel** tape is normally recorded and played back at either 7½ ips or 15 ips, and very occasionally at 30 ips. This faster speed allows easier **editing**; the faster the tape travels the more there is of it to play with. Audio-**cassette** tape is recorded and played back more slowly – hence poorer quality but less bulk.

iris (*film*) a variable diaphragm on a camera lens, rather like the iris of a human eye. You can move it so it creates the effect of a circle of increasing or decreasing diameter.

iron (*BT*) in traditional theatre the fireproof or safety curtain.

J

jingle (*sound*) a short piece of music that advertises a product or service, usually used for television or radio commercials.

jitter (*VT*) the effect created by a videotape picture that jumps about when it's played back. Possibly caused by poor-quality or worn tape.

jump cut (*VT, film*) a **cut** from one scene to another where there is a hiccup in **continuity**, e.g. a shot of someone in New York immediately followed by a shot of the same person in Paris. Avoided by inserting a **cutaway** in the middle, perhaps – say a shot of an airliner in mid flight.

jumper (*all*) a cable with a selection of different connections, for powering equipment.

junk (*ST, film, VT, sound*) to throw something away, usually a programme, film or recording which has become obsolete.

J

K

Kensington gore (*VT*, *film*) from the street in London. Fake blood and gore, used for appropriately macabre dramatisations.

keyer (*VT*) in videotape **editing**, a device which effectively creates a 'hole' in the screen image so a **caption** or other content can be added in.

key grip (*VT*, *film*) the most senior general handyman (handyperson) on the crew.
   See also **grip**

key light (*VT*, *film*, *sound*) the main light on a **set** or **location**; often the first to be set up. Other lighting is then brought in to supplement it appropriately.

keystone (*BT*, *ST*) the correct angle for projection, which in theory is bang opposite the screen. However when you have several projectors pointing at the same place on screen, some – especially the outer ones – will be at a slightly different angle. This means the projected image becomes trapezoidal. Special lenses can compensate for this, but nevertheless you can expect to hear much swearing and cursing when projectors are being lined up – it's always tricky.

kill (*BT*) an instruction given by whoever is **calling** the **show**. It means to deactivate whatever follows.
   See also **go**

knockdown (*VT*, *film*) a portable collapsible dressing room for performers to use on **location**.

L

lace up (*film, sound*) to **thread** film through a **projector** or sound-tape around a recorder. In the case of film, projection is the only possible outcome, but with sound-tape you lace up the machine before either recording or playback.

landscape format (*ST*) in original 35 mm photography this means holding the camera the right way up, i.e. horizontally, rather than turning it round 90° to the vertical or **portrait** format. Slide–tape photography is always done in landscape format, as that is the way in which the slides are always projected.

lapel mike (*VT, film, BT*) a small **microphone** which clips on to a lapel or other suitably placed article of clothing. The wire will pass through the clothing and out of sight along the floor. Alternatively, in the case of a **radio microphone**, the wire will go down under the jacket to a small transmitter which you wear clipped or strapped to your back. The radio version requires care and attention when you sit down.

launch (*BT*) an event where a new product or service is introduced to the audience for the first time. Some companies spend a great deal of money on launches, with all the spectacular tricks of the business theatre trade thrown in. Others will be very much more modest.

lavender (*film, sound*) positive film **stock** which you use to make duplicates. Also refers to a print actually made from this stock.

laying back (*VT, sound*) a sound **editing** or **mixing** term. It means to finalise all your different sound **tracks**, all at the right levels for the final **mix** on to the **master** tape.

laying it down (*sound*) the act of recording something.

leader (*film, sound*) a length of blank non-recordable film or tape on the front end of a **reel**, to use for **lacing up** before **playback**.

lectern (*BT*) the stand or box at which a speaker stands while delivering his or her speech. There will be one or two **microphones** attached to it; if a **teleprompter** is being used, that will be installed in the lectern as well. There will also be somewhere for the speaker to put notes, if needed, and sometimes a glass of water.

lenser (*film*) the director of photography.

lensing (*film*) the act of making a film.

letterbox (*VT*) a rectangle at the bottom of the picture, electronically generated. In this, using a **cap gen** machine, you can insert whatever words you like underneath the main image.

level (*sound*) strictly speaking, level can refer to the level of anything – volume, bass, treble, etc. However in common parlance we talk about level when we mean volume – the amount of noise.

library film (*VT, film*) film sequences which are rented from a specialist library, e.g. panoramic views of a city, shots of a type of animal, etc. You then incorporate what you want of that into your own programme or film and pay the library a fee.
See also **stock shot**

library music (*all*) 'off the peg' music, rather than 'tailor made' music composed specially. There are several music libraries in the UK and most other Western countries, all offering LP records of various types of music – nearly all instrumental. The music has been recorded in carefully-timed segments for easy editing. You can use this kind of music for almost any kind of production – even for broadcast. The fees you pay for using it vary according to the amount and the purpose for which it will be used.

111

library stills (*ST*) the same principle as **library film**. If you're making a **programme** and want a **shot** of a specific object or place, rather than sending a photographer out at high cost to shoot it, you can hire it in from a library. You then **dupe** a copy off the original, using a **rostrum camera**, and return the original to the library. Plus their fee, of course . . .

See also **stock shot**

lightbox (*ST*) a box, table or wall panel with a translucent cover and fluorescent lights inside. Slides can be placed or clipped on the cover and viewed easily, with plenty of light coming from beneath or behind.

lightbox preview (*ST, BT*) clients can get an update on how their **show** or **module** is coming together by viewing the slides on a **lightbox**. The slides will either be laid out on **trays** or will be standing on little ridges in front of a wall-mounted lightbox. In this way they can be seen in presentation order.

lighting (*BT*) tends to be more complicated than traditional theatre lighting as it must be bright and effective without interfering with whatever is going on on the screen. Also, some **venues** don't lend themselves to a conventional stage **set**, so lights have to be strung up from the most awkward places. Objects like decorative mirrors and elaborate chandeliers are frequent occupational hazards, too.

lighting cameraman (*film*) the most senior cameraman; also called a **cinematographer**.

lighting design (*BT*) the process of assessing the **venue**, the **set** and the requirements of a show, then drawing a plan indicating where all the lights should be placed and what lights should be used.

lighting designer (*BT*) the person who designs and implements the **lighting** for a show. Like many people in business theatre (and conventional theatre – many lighting designers work in both areas) the lighting designer has a rare combination of creative talent and technical expertise. He or she must combine technical wisdom with a lot of artistic flair in order to create the best possible visual effects within what are often highly restrictive circumstances.

lighting rigger (*BT*) someone who usually helps the **lighting designer** put up and run the lights for a **show**. Sometimes, though, if the lighting designer can't be around during rigging the lighting rigger will **rig** the lights him or herself, according to the designer's detailed plan.

lime (*BT*) a ·general nickname for a light, particularly a **spotlight**.

line up (*ST, BT*) to line up means to adjust your projectors so that they are all in focus and pointing at the same area on screen. Special line-up slides, with grids designed in, are used for maximum precision. The line-up, as a compound noun, is the state of all the projectors' focus and accuracy.

linear (*VT*) an expression used to describe a videotape programme where the viewer's only participation is to watch it – i.e. a straightforward **playback** programme. Often used to differentiate between ordinary and **inter-active** programmes; a linear programme is non-inter-active.

link (*all*) any live or pre-recorded **sequence** that leads the audience or viewers from the main topic to the next.

lip mike (*VT, film*) a **microphone** consisting of a fine strip of metal, working on a magnetic principle, which is held near the speaker's mouth. Also called a ribbon mike.

lip sync (*VT, film*) when you simultaneously hear and see someone speak on screen. The sound will usually be recorded at the same time as taping or filming. In the case of film, though, the performer may well **dub** his or her words on later in the studio – **location** sound recording quality is seldom as good as the **studio** variety.

lith (*ST*) short for lithographic, this is line film which produces a negative result. If your original **artwork** consists of black letters on white paper, the final slide photographed on lith will show clear (transparent) letters on a black background. On screen, this will project as white letters on a black background. By adding a coloured **gel** into the slide, along with the lith film, the otherwise white letters are projected on screen in the colour of the gel. The lith can be re-photographed with a colour to achieve this same effect, as part of a **colour conversion** process in slide making. Similarly, artwork on lith (in monochrome) is re-photographed along with special effects such as **neon**, using the **rostrum camera**. The results project as colourfully illustrated and/or highlighted words and figures on screen.

live (*all*)
(**1**) something is live when it is turned on and ready for use, e.g. a live **microphone** as opposed to a dead mike (switched off).
(**2**) live also means actually happening now, as opposed to a pre-recorded production, e.g. a live business theatre speech or a live television or radio broadcast.

live action (*VT, film*) a production with real human activity, as opposed to **animation** (cartoon), **graphics**, **special effects**, etc.

load (*all*) to put your **software** into the **hardware**. You load a stills or movie camera with film; you load a recording machine with audio tape; you load a **projector** with a **magazine** of slides, etc.

location (*ST, VT, film, sound*) any place outside a **studio** where photography, taping, filming or sound recording is done; any work that involves a **crew** travelling away from home base, either indoors or out.

lock (*all*) to ensure that all equipment is running properly and in **sync**.

lock down (*ST*) usually used in the phrase 'lock down sequence'. In the **studios**, or on **location**, the camera is placed on a tripod and then locked down into position. It will have a **zoom lens** on it. Then, a **sequence** of shots is taken, zooming the lens in by a measured distance each time. The end result

L

is a sequence of shots of the same object, each one showing a bit nearer the camera lens. The effect can also be done using a **rostrum camera**. The term lock down can also be used to describe other effects created by using a camera firmly anchored in place; e.g. simulated movement, such as shots of the various stages of a parcel being unwrapped.

loft (*film*, *VT*, *BT*) the area of a studio or theatre right at the top of the performing area above the **grid**.

logo (*VT*, *film*, *BT*, *ST*) a design or symbol which represents a company's name or corporate image. Sometimes it will just be the company's name in a specified typeface, in other cases it will be a symbol plus the name.

long shot (*VT*, *film*, *ST*) *see* **shot lengths**

long tom (*ST*, *VT*, *film*) very high-powered telephoto-type of lens for long-distance work.

loop (*sound*) a piece of tape that's made into a loop and **played back** through special equipment. Gives a continuous sound for however long you need. Useful for **sound effects**.

lose (*BT*, *sound*) to deactivate a piece of equipment; an alternative to **kill**.

lot (*VT*, *film*) comes from the American word meaning piece of land (or plot in the UK). An area adjacent to a VT or film **studio** where you can build and use **sets**.

low band (*VT*) a ¾-inch-wide videotape format. Very seldom used as the **master** taping format as the quality isn't quite up to it. However the quality is better than the domestic formats of **VHS** and **Betamax**, and low band is often used for business use **playback**.
See also **high band, U-matic**

low loader (*VT*, *film*) a low, flat, wheeled trailer. The camera **crew** sits on it so that they can **shoot** the interior of the vehicle that's towing it. Can be a pretty tricky way to earn a living, especially when you're trying to shoot a high-speed car chase.

LS (*VT*, *film*, *ST*) stands for long shot.
See also **shot lengths**

L

macky (*VT*, *film*, *BT*) slang for stage makeup. Probably from the French word for it, *maquillage*.

mag (*ST*, *film*) abbreviation for **magazine**.

magazine (*ST*, *film*) container, normally circular, for slides, placed on top of the **projector**, e.g. a **Carousel**. Also a container for film, either in the camera or projector. Sometimes shortened to mag.

make-off (*BT*) the **flats** furthest **downstage** nearest the audience and to the extreme left and right of the **set**. In this business, a make-off either side of the set is a very helpful way of hiding all the chaos and confusion going on **backstage**.

M & E track (*film*) stands for music and effects track, which will be **dubbed** on to a film at **editing** stage. The dialogue will be on a separate **track** at this point.

mark it (*film*) an instruction, usually yelled out to whoever is operating the **clapperboard**. It means that he or she should operate the clapperboard in order to indicate on film the beginning of the next **take**.

married print (*film*) *see* **combined print**

mask (*ST*, *film*) with slides, masks – made from **lith** film or thin metal – can be incorporated into the slide **mount** in order to mask off part of the image. This gives interesting effects on screen, particularly when you're using several **projectors**. With film, similar results can be obtained from masking, but in this case it has to be done in the laboratory using special equipment.

master (*ST*, *VT*, *film*, *sound*) the final, finished article when all **editing**, polishing or **mixing** has been completed. The master copy in any of these categories is the one from which all other copies will be made.

master shot (*VT*, *film*) the main framework of a particular **sequence**. For example, in an **interview** the master shot would be of the interview itself. Afterwards, **cutaways** illustrating various points the speaker makes could be added at **editing** stage. In a dramatic sequence the master shot would be of all performers doing their bits together. **Close-up**, **reverse angles** and so on would be shot afterwards (the actors having to do it all again) and edited in later.

matrix (*ST*, *BT*) a picture (or the format used to build it) which is made of several different **masked** slides.

matt (*film*) a process not unlike colour separation overlay (**CSO**), except this is the film equivalent. A performer will be filmed against a non-reflective background. Another **scene**, e.g. mountains, countryside, wild horses galloping, or even cartoon characters leaping about, can then be added on in the non-reflective background areas. The end result is that the two bits of live **action** or **animation** are combined and look like one scene.

MCU (*VT*, *film*, *ST*) stands for medium close up.
  See also **shot lengths**

MD (*sound*) acronym for musical director. Someone who directs and conducts the performers during the recording of music. He or she may also be the **arranger** of the music, and possibly may have composed the music.

meeting (*BT*) a conference or presentation; usually refers to the smaller variety.

memory (*ST*) as in computers. In fact most **programming** in slide–tape work is done using small computers up to micro size. Slide **cues** in a slide–tape programme can be retained in the memory of the relevant machine, then dumped on disk for use later.

mice (*BT*) **microphones** placed on stage near the **footlights**.

Mickey Mouse (*film*) a soundtrack style, developed from early cartoons, where the music exactly follows everything that goes on in vision.

microphone (*all*) voice, music or sound amplification device that permits a multitude of wonders to be worked. There are a great many types of different microphone available, covered in separate entries. One word of advice, though; never blow into microphones to see if they're **live** or when doing a sound check. If you do you're likely to see the sound engineer turn purple – the moisture from your breath can wreak havoc with the delicate innards of some mikes. Tap the mike gently instead.
   See also **boom, directional mike, lapel mike, lip mike, mice, neck mike, omni-directional mike, radio mike, rifle mike**

microvideo (*VT*) an extremely small video-cassette format. The tapes themselves are only slightly bigger than audio cassettes, and the **playback** units, with a tiny **monitor** built in, are about the size of a ladies' handbag. Cute, but not much use for audiences bigger than one.

middle eight (*sound*) originally the central eight musical bars in a piece of music that break up the mainstream musical thought of the song. Usually different, and contrasting with the main melody. Nowadays the middle eight may well consist of rather more than eight bars, but the name has stuck.

mike (*sound*) abbreviation for **microphone**.

mike up (*sound, BT*) to arrange, plug in and adjust **microphones**. Usually pertains to performers, e.g. (to a **voice-over** artiste) 'Could you go and sit down in the **sound booth** now as we'd like to mike you up.'

mix (*VT, film, sound*)
(1) in vision terms, this is a slightly faster version of a **dissolve** – a gentle transition from one picture to the next by **fading** the last one down as you bring the next one up.
(2) in sound, the mix is when all the individual **tracks** are recorded and blended together on one **master** tape. This will normally involve a great deal of **tweaking** of **levels** and sound quality, especially if the recording is of a piece of music.

mix down (*sound*) another way of saying to **mix**. When you've completed and assembled all your individual tracks, you mix them down into the final **master**.

MLS (*VT, film, ST*) stands for medium long shot.
See also **shot lengths**

mobile unit (*or* **OB unit** *or* **scanner**) (*VT*) a small television or videotape recording **studio** built into a large truck. These trucks are used mostly for live broadcasts of events like football games, outdoor concerts and so on, and can activate live transmission to millions of viewers. However you might well hire one of these to tape a large event, even if there were no broadcast requirements. If you were using several cameras, each one would have a **monitor** link with the mobile unit, allowing you to keep tabs on what all the cameras were doing. A **director** physically trying to run eight cameras placed, say, round an eighteen-hole golf course, would drive him or herself mad without a mobile.
See also **OB**

mode (*all*) computerese for 'function' or 'fashion'. For example, videotape machinery could be in record mode or playback mode.

module (*ST, BT*) a free-standing slide–tape or **multi-image** programme with pre-recorded **soundtrack**. In business theatre you differentiate between modules and the **speaker support** slides, which have no sound and are manually **cued**. Modules are driven by the electronic **pulses** put on one **track** of the audio tape. You'll also hear modules referred to as **AVs**, but technically this is wrong.

Mongolian (*VT, film*) *see* **Chinese**

monitor (*VT, BT*) any 'television set' which is not used to pick up broadcast TV signals. Some monitors, like those in a videotape **editing suite**, physically can't pick up broadcast – they're designed purely for tape **playback**. Similarly, the monitors used in **teleprompter** devices can only do the one job – transmit the script as picked up by the closed circuit camera. However, if you have a normal TV set in your home or office and it's plugged into a videocassette recorder, that set is functioning as a monitor, although it's capable of doing both jobs. *See also* **CCTV**

monkey fist (*VT, film*) a bit of rope or other suitable material that hangs from a microphone **boom**. The idea is to stop people from walking into the boom and hurting themselves, or the **shot**.

mono (*sound*) sound that has been recorded through one single input track, sound which is played back through one single output source, or both. **Stereo** or even **quadrophonic** sound can be played back over mono equipment, although some quality is lost.

montage (*all*) any compilation of several pictures or sounds, filmed or recorded so that it appears as one **sequence**.

MOR (*sound*) stands for middle of (the) road. A term used to describe 'easy listening' music which is innocuous and non-controversial in style.

MOS (*VT, film*) a **script** instruction, that the particular scene in question should be taped or filmed without sound. The full, unabbreviated version, 'mit out sound', is said to have been coined by a German director who couldn't speak English properly.

mosaic (*ST*) a way of designing overlaid grids so that two pictures can be projected together and appear to come up in alternate 'boxes' or 'holes' on screen.

motor drive (*ST*) a battery-powered unit either built in or bolted on to a stills camera. It automatically winds the film on inside the camera each time the photographer has pressed the shutter. Sophisticated cameras, with a combination of motor drive and a repeat action shutter, can shoot rapid sequences of stills – say perhaps six or seven **shots** of a horse and rider jumping over a fence. These types of action **sequences** work very well in **multi-image** programmes – not quite motion pictures, but an interesting effect that gives a strong impression of movement.

mount (*ST*) a plastic and glass contraption in which a **35 mm** transparency is placed; this constitutes a slide ready for **programming** into a **projector**. The mount is normally hinged at the top; inside there are little knobs placed so that the **sprocket** holes on the bare film will fit over them tightly. This means the film inside stays put. You then close the mount, bringing the hinged top down, and it clips shut, with the glass 'windows' front and back allowing full view of the image inside.

move left/right (*VT*, *film*) a camera instruction. Means the same as to **crab** left or right – moving sideways without swivelling.

Moviola (*film*) the brand name for a type of viewing and **editing** machine. Used sometimes as a general term for film editing machines.

MS (*VT*, *film*, *ST*) stands for medium shot.
  See also **shot lengths**

multicam (*VT*, *film*) abbreviation for multi-camera. Any **scene** or **production** that requires several cameras so that every possible angle is covered without doing umpteen takes and shifting a single camera each time.
  See also **EFP**

multi-image (*ST*, *BT*) the American word for any slide–tape programme that involves the use of three or more **projectors**. Used widely in the UK now, as well, although the Brits used to call it **multivision**.

multi-media (*BT*) using more than one medium in all or any part of a live show. For example, you can combine slide projection with videotape or film projection, extra **sound effects**, **smoke machines**, **dry ice fog**, etc.

multiplane (*film*) a cartoon or **animation** technique whereby you can create the impression of depth by subtle spacing of foreground, middle ground and background. The traditional way was to put each layer on a separate **cell**.

multiplexer (*ST, VT*) an ingenious system which is used to transfer **multi-image** slide–tape programmes to videotape. With a clever system of mirrors or prisms, placing **projectors** around the four sides of a square and using a special videotape camera, you get a very good, sharp image. Of course, the slide–tape programme has to have been made in a single-**screen** format to start with, and all its slides should have been made **TV safe**.

multi-projector (*ST, BT*) any **programme** that requires more than three **projectors**.

multi-screen (*ST, BT*) some people get this term mixed up with **multi-image** and **multi-projector**, and use it freely in these contexts. However, multi-screen means just that – more than one screen. To create a panoramic effect, you can project more than one 35 mm slide equivalent – you can have two, three, five, seven or even nine. Obviously you need a lot of projectors to keep all those screen areas busy. There will probably only be one actual screen; in this context, you're talking about the projection area rather than the physical number of screens. Mind you, if you get up to five, seven or nine screen areas you *will* need to put up more than one real screen – and put them in a curved shape, too, which causes bad headaches to whoever is doing the **line-up**. A popular compromise in business theatre is to use a combination; a two-screen area with an extra one across the middle for a featured effect, for example – three into two.

multi-track (*sound*) the capability, and the process, of recording several different sounds separately and then knitting them together into one **master** tape. The purpose of this is so

123

that you can adjust all the **levels** as much as you want at the **mix** stage. You also get a much purer, controllable sound if each section is recorded separately, e.g. **narration**, **sound effects**, music. When you consider a piece of music played by twenty different instruments, plus three or four singers, the good sense of multi-tracking becomes even more obvious. With music, multi-tracking is usually done in chunks rather than taking each individual instrument one at a time. For example, you might record stringed instruments first, then brass and woodwinds, then guitars, then percussion and piano. Lastly, when the instrumental **track** – a collective term in this instance – is finished you add the vocals. The singers would listen to the instrumental track through their **cans** and sing along with it into their **microphones**. Recording **studios** that are used for industrial or business work tend to be on the small side, with a multi-track capability of four or eight separate tracks. Music studios, though, start at eight or sixteen tracks and go up to twenty-four, thirty-two, forty-eight and even sixty-four individual recording tracks on offer. And the tapes these big studios use are huge – up to 3 inches wide – in order to get all the tracks on to one tape.

multivision (*ST*, *BT*) the British word for any slide–tape programme that involves the use of three or more **projectors**. Now largely replaced by the American word, **multi-image**.

mummerset (*VT*, *film*, *sound*) the phoney rural accents often adopted by actors. They always sound as though they come from the West Country of England, hence the combination of mummer and Somerset.

music (*all*) an important addition to almost any **production**. Creates interest and helps to augment the mood of the **script**. Can be either composed specially for the job, which is expensive, or selected from a wide range of **library music** available in most Western countries.

M

musical director (*sound*) *see* **MD**

music composition (*all*) an expensive but highly effective way of getting precisely the right musical backing for a **production**. **Library music** is the cheaper alternative.

    See also **composer**

music selection (*all*) the process you go through in order to find the best **library music** for a **production**. Who makes the selection depends on who's best at it among the **crew** members. Most music libraries employ researchers who know many of the **tracks** by heart, and certainly know the results each record is likely to give. They can pre-select five or six albums for you to listen to, provided you brief them properly. Sound **engineers** in recording studios usually know where to look, too.

mute (*film*) any print of a film that has no **soundtrack** incorporated in it.

N

narration (*all*) a narration is a scripted **commentary** (commentary is strictly speaking supposed to be **ad libbed**, as in sports commentating). Narrations provide voices which are heard but not seen, usually, but some techniques do involve a **narrator** performing **to camera** for part of the time at least. Some people say **voice over** when they mean narration, but in fact the voice over is a sound term rather than a **script** term.

narrator (*all*) the person who speaks a **narration** – a very skilled job, requiring a good microphone voice. The top narrators and **voice over** artistes in this business are usually actors or television journalists and a few have a background in radio.

narrowcast (*VT*) not surprisingly, the opposite of **broadcast**. Sometimes used to describe broadcast transmissions on TV and radio destined for small specialist audiences. Also widely used to describe the sort of videotape work done in this business, whether it's broadcast or not.

National Television Systems Committee (*VT*) *see* **NTSC**

neck mike (*VT, film, sound, BT*) a small **microphone** which you hang around the performer's neck. For all intents and purposes the rest of its function is like that of a **lapel mike**.

neon (*ST*) particularly bright-coloured **special effect** on slide, often used to highlight a word or other image on screen.

news magazine (*VT, film*) a style of programme used a lot in this business, and pinched directly from television news programmes around the world. It's a good way of getting over a selection of bits of information to viewers, mixing up short items with longer interviews. The style is used predominantly for in-company communications – head office producing, say, a half-hour VT programme once every few weeks or months and sending copies to all its branches. It's a very good way of keeping even the far-flung factories in touch with what's going on elsewhere in the company. The format usually consists of a studio **anchor** presenter who gives the main headlines and introduces each featured item, plus a collection of **narrated** news items that are edited in.

newsreader voice (*sound*) a factual, non-emotional style of **narration**. Some say the best **voice-over** artistes to do a newsreader voice are non-actors as thespians always manage to work in a bit of drama, no matter how much they try to keep it straight.

Newton's rings (*ST*) the contoured rings you sometimes see in projection when a **transparency** has been mounted in a cheap or defective slide **mount**. The effect is caused when the shiny side of the film presses up against untreated glass in the mount.

noddies (*VT, film*) a way of making an **interview** shot with one camera look as though it has been done with two. After the main interview has been finished, with the camera on the interviewee all that time, you then **shoot** a few angles of the interviewer 'listening' to the interviewee – who's probably off to the canteen by then. The interviewer smiles, looks intent and nods – hence the nickname. These shots are then edited into the interview later on, **cut** in here and there while the interviewee's voice is heard **OOV**. Sometimes, if the interviewer has not performed too well during the interview, the **director** will shoot his or her questions again, as well.

non-theatrical (*all*) in the movie business this is how you describe all films which are shown for free – to charity groups, school children, etc. – and all 16 mm films. The term is also used to describe business/industrial types of work, although this can be somewhat inaccurate; some of these productions, especially in business theatre, are very theatrical indeed.

NTSC (*VT*) stands for National Television Systems Committee. This is the television system used all over North America and in Japan. It operates on the basis of 525 lines, as opposed to the European systems of **PAL** and **SECAM**, which are based on 625 lines.

O

O

OB (*VT*) stands for outside broadcast. Normally involves a **mobile unit** and means that a live television show can be transmitted from wherever the unit is. Although in this business there is seldom any involvement with broadcasting, there may still occasionally be a call for an outside broadcast unit (a TV studio built into a large truck).

obie (*VT, film*) a small light with around 250 watts of power. Sits on the camera mounting so it can be pointed at a specific performer or object.

off-camera (*VT, film*) any **narration** or other performance which is heard but not seen on screen, e.g. an off-camera interviewer – you hear the questions asked but only see the interviewee.

off-line edit (*VT*) when editing videotape, the process of viewing and deciding on which sections of tape you're going to use for the **on-line edit**. If you're not well prepared this process can take days – at high cost. One way of reducing off-lining time is to write down each **take** of each **shot** you do when actually taping your programme, and mark down which takes you will use. Working from a detailed **storyboard** will also help, as you'll already know which pictures you'll use with which words. In shorter programmes, off-lining and on-lining are often done in the same session, but it's nearly always the off-lining that takes the time.

off script (*BT*) a speaker is off script when he or she **ad libs**. Unless the ad lib has been decided on beforehand and the **crew** have been warned, that's when mild panic sets in in the projection area.
   See also **on script**

129

O

offstage (*BT*) any activity which takes place away from the stage but which has a direct bearing on what's going on there, e.g. offstage mike announcements are announcements made by someone over a **live microphone**, usually from the projection area or other convenient spot. The announcements are heard but the speaker is not seen and is therefore offstage.

off-the-shelf-module (*BT*) some business theatre production companies make **themed modules** for use in any of their clients' **shows**, which can either be used on their own or slightly tailored to fit the client's needs. Examples of this would be modules on how to make a sale, how to deal with a difficult customer, how to work a word processor, the basics of retail advertising or point of sale, etc. The advantage to clients is that the cost is much lower than if the module were made specifically for them; the advantage to production companies is that such modules can be re-used many times.

OHP (*BT*) stands for **overhead projector**.

omni-directional mike (*sound*) a microphone that picks up sound from all directions.
    See also **directional mike**

on a bell (*film*) on a film **set** a bell is sometimes rung shortly before filming starts. To be on a bell means that the bell has rung and **action** is imminent.

on-camera (*VT, film*) in theory any performance which takes place in front of the camera lens. In practice, usually used to refer to an interviewer or presenter who appears on screen while doing his or her bit, as distinct from **off-camera** interviews and **voice-over** presentations.

1 inch (*VT*) a videotape format. Technically it is considered to be of broadcast standard and some television programmes are shot and **mastered** on 1 inch, although **2 inch** is generally considered best. For this business though, 1 inch is plenty good enough; indeed it is often too expensive actually to **shoot** with. What frequently happens is that programmes are shot on **BVU (high band)** and then transferred to 1 inch for **editing** and mastering. This means **crew** members don't get hernias carrying the heavier 1 inch cameras around and you don't cripple your budget either. The end result, with 1 inch quality of editing, is excellent.

See also **low band, U-matic**

O

one-legged (*VT, sound*) less than perfect quality of sound, particularly in the case of television or radio transmission.

one-shot (*or* **single**) (*VT, film*) any **shot** or **sequence** where there is only one performer in view.

on-line edit (*VT*) when **editing** videotape, the process of re-recording the selected sections of tape straight on to the **master**. This is done after the **off-line edit**.

on-screen preview (*ST, BT*) the next stage in the course of production after a **light-box preview**, where a client can see his or her slides. In the case of slide–tape **modules**, the **soundtrack** and rough programming will have been done so the client can watch the projected module almost as it will appear on the day. Obviously there will be a few **write-on** or **Ektographic** slides replacing the real things in the **magazines** as there will still be some final slides in the process of being made, mounted, etc.

on script (*BT*) a speaker is on script when he or she is sticking to the written words.
See also **ad lib, off script**

OOV (*VT, film*) stands for out of vision. Usually refers to a performer who can be heard but not seen, if only for a line or two.

open reel (*VT, sound*) *see* **reel-to-reel**

opticals (*film*) the whole range of visual effects (other than **live action**, which is shot in the normal way) which is put on film in the laboratory.

optical sound (*film*) the way in which sound is put on to **16**

131

O

mm and **35 mm** film. It's put on photographically and then played back via a photocell.

orchestra stall (*BT*) in a conventional theatre the orchestra stalls are the seats at the very front, near the stage, or just behind the area where the orchestra would be.

OS (*VT*, *film*) stands for over the shoulder.
  See also **over-the-shoulder shot**

oscar (*VT*, *film*) a device that diffuses light. It's made in four sections so you can use all four to vary the direction and intensity of the light.

out cue (*VT*, *BT*, *sound*) a **cue** in the script, or in what a performer says, to indicate that the programme or performance is about to end.
  See also **outro**

outline (*or* **synopsis**) (*ST*, *VT*, *film*) a brief general overview of how a proposed production will look and sound. The outline is usually the first stage of production and will present the bare bones of the ideas for discussion between client and **production company**. From there, once the outline is agreed, you proceed to a **treatment** and, after that, to a full **script**.

out of rack (*film*) when a film is projected it can sometimes come adrift from the **sprockets** that hold it in place while going through the **gate**. When this happens you'll often see the film edges projected on screen. This is when a film is out of **rack**.

out of vision (*VT*, *film*) *see* **OOV**

outro (*all*) the opposite of **intro**. An outro is the wind-up in the **script** of a **narration**, **interview**, speech or whatever, and serves as a **cue** for the **crew** that the end is nigh.

out-takes (*VT*, *film*, *sound*) the bits of videotape, film or audio tape which are not used in the final **master**, for whatever reason. Very often out-takes include scenes which have gone wrong, with **effects** not working, performers getting their lines

overhead projector

wrong and cursing in a highly undignified manner, etc. Needless to say the funnier out-takes are frequently pirated out of studios all over the world, and provide hours of hilarious entertainment. In fact, some out-takes find their way on to broadcast television screens as comedy shows or items in their own right.
See also **POT**

overcrank (*film*) to run a camera faster than the normal speed of twenty-four frames per second. If the resulting film is projected at normal speed, the screen effect will be **slow motion**. You can also overcrank a projector, which will speed up a normally-shot film. The opposite effect is **undercranking**. The whole business of cranking comes from the days when both cameras and projectors were cranked by hand, rather than electrically driven.

overdub (*sound*) to add extra sounds – effects, additional vocals, etc. – to an existing recording.
See also **double track, multi-track**

overhead projector (*BT*) the *bête noire* of the business theatre **producer**, and the pet of many high-ranking conference speakers. An overhead projector consists of a machine that projects, via a system of mirrors, etc., an image which is being drawn or shown on a lighted lectern. The projection device is such that it projects the image over the speaker's head and on to the screen or wall behind – hence the name. Speakers like OHPs because they can draw their own particular hieroglyphics and have them instantly projected, as well as being able to show pre-drawn or written slides. The problem **producers** have with OHPs is that the quality of the projected image is very poor, with bad definition and pale, washy colour. Speakers' presentations look a hundred times more professional if the slides are thought out beforehand, professionally created, shot on **35 mm** and projected by a professional **programmer**, leaving the speaker just to get on with the speech. OHP presentations are frequently stilted and patchy, with long silences while the speaker draws a chart or hunts around in a briefcase for a missing word slide. To make matters worse, an OHP presentation mixed in with other presentations using 35 mm slides looks like a very poor country cousin; 35 mm slides will beat

133

the pants off **overhead projector slides** for quality every time. All the same, the overhead projector still has its devotees.

overhead projector slide (*BT*) a **slide** several inches square, allowing plenty of space for drawing or writing on clear celluloid.

See also **overhead projector**

overs (*BT, ST*) slides which are mounted up but not actually used in the production. The slide version of **out-takes**.

over-the-shoulder shot (*VT, film*) the camera is behind the performer, shooting over his or her shoulder with the shoulder in shot. A popular technique for the introductory shot in an **interview**, with the camera behind the interviewer's shoulder pointing at the interviewee.

P

PA (*BT, sound, VT, film*) in the outside world a PA can be a personal assistant, i.e. a senior secretary, while in the entertainment, theatre and movie world a PA can be either a press agent or a publicity agent. However in this business a PA will be one of the following.
(1) a public address system.
(2) a **production assistant**.

pack shot (*ST, VT, film*) any photograph, still or moving, of the client's product.

Paganini (*film*) a system of graded blocks developed by Italian film **crews**. This allows the camera to be raised and lowered quickly and efficiently.

Paintbox (*VT*) a **computer generated graphics** system made by **Quantel**. This very sophisticated system can create in minutes what an art studio or film laboratory would do in several days; it has a highly impressive range of functions. It also costs a great deal of money, which limits its cost-effectiveness to all but the very large and/or dedicated user. Of course, this is how it is at the time of writing; as technology improves the capital cost of such machinery may well become more accessible to smaller companies in the business.

paintpot (*VT, film*) an electronic device on a **telecine** machine which the operator can use to make changes to the colour ranges of the film, either during transmission, in the case of TV, or during transfer to videotape.

PAL (*VT*) acronym for phase alternate line. This is the tele-

135

vision system used in the UK and most of Western Europe except France. It's based on a 625-line structure.
See also **NTSC, PAL M, SECAM**

PAL M (*VT*) a variation on the **PAL** TV format. This uses only 525 lines rather than the 625 lines used in the PAL format of the UK and most of Europe. PAL M is used in Brazil.
See also **NTSC, SECAM**

P

pan (*VT*, *film*) a camera instruction. Means that the camera should swivel left or right on its mounting, with the **tripod** or **dolly** staying put.

pancake (*VT*, *film*) for short performers. A piece of wood to stand on, hidden from the camera's beady eye, which raises them up to a suitably awe-inspiring height (provided they don't walk away into the sunset).

panic button (*BT*) for speakers who aren't too sure of their slide **cues** in the **script**, or who **ad lib** a speech. Pressing the panic button on the lectern activates the **cue light** in the projection area and tells the **programmer** that the next slide is needed.

panning handle (*VT*, *film*) an arm attached to the camera mounting which the cameraman can use to move the camera around, especially to **pan** the camera left and right or to **tilt** it up or down.

panpot (*sound*) acronym for panoramic potentiometer (no wonder it's abbreviated). A device which, by changing the signal strength from each of several sound speakers in sequence, can make sound appear to move around. Useful **special effect** for business theatre spectaculars.

paste-up (*ST*) the normal method of assembling human-generated **artwork** for a word or chart slide. The various elements of the slide, e.g. strips of **typeset** words and numbers, are pasted on to the paper or **cell** in suitable positions.

pedestal (*VT*) in transmission or videotape **playback**, this

is the voltage level that is pertinent to the black tones on screen.
See also **picture black**

per diem (*all*) the daily cash for expenses paid out to **crews** when on **location** or at business theatre events.

persuader (*VT*) an electrode in a TV tube. This deflects the returning beam of scanning electrons back into the electron multiplier.

P

PFL (*sound*) stands for **pre-fade listen**.

phase alternate line (*VT*) *see* **PAL**

photographer (*ST*) a great many print photographers have jumped on the **AV** bandwagon in the last few years, knowing a good thing when they see it. However, I don't believe that any print photographer can start doing AV photography without learning about the techniques first. So beware – it's always safer to hire specialist AV photographers who understand the nature of slide–tape work and who won't bring you back half the shots in **portrait format** and a whole collection of single, one-off photographs (highly unsuitable for AV).
See also **photography**

photography (*ST*) the stills photography required to produce **35 mm slides** for this business is highly skilled and somewhat different to the zany, finger-clicking stuff you might see in a fashion studio. For a start, one golden rule is that you never turn your camera round to do **portrait formats**; always, always use **landscape format**. And you need to think in **sequences** of **shots** rather than in single shots.
See also **photographer**

photomatic (*VT, film*) a way of making a **demo** of a programme or film – usually a television commercial. Unlike an **animatic**, which is a taped or filmed version of the drawn **storyboard**, a photomatic uses still photographs of models, packs, etc. Usually the pictures are synchronised to a demo **soundtrack** for a more realistic feel, then videotaped.

P

picture black (*VT*) the light strength of the darkest bit of a TV picture, or the corresponding picture signal voltage.

pilot (*VT, sound*) in broadcast television a pilot programme is a one-off effort that acts as a sample of a series or serial yet to be made. In this business, though, the word pilot is used rather as is the word **demo** – a cheaply-produced production or sound recording to give clients an idea of what the real thing would be like, without going to the full expense.

pinboard (*ST*) a drawing board used for doing **registered artwork**.

pin registration (*ST, film*) is a method used to get absolutely accurate placing of transparency photographs which eventually become slides. Special cameras have pins placed in the back to fit exactly in the **sprocket holes** of the film to be exposed. This holds the film firmly in place without the slightest risk of even marginal movement. Corresponding pins in the **slide mounts** ensure that the image is in the right place when the slide is projected. Pin registration is used to create special slide effects, especially multiple exposures; the film can be exposed several times over, with each new image or effect in precisely the right place. The technique was originally developed for **animation** (cartoon) work on film, where several sequential drawings are photographed in exactly the same location on consecutive film frames. This creates the effect of smooth motion.

plastic (*BT*) any scenery or part of the **set** which has three dimensions, as opposed to the two-dimensional **flats**.

playback (*VT, sound*) is the act of running a **programme** or **soundtrack** for viewing purposes, after it has been recorded. This can be in the studio, where immediate playback can take place; or it can refer to the end-viewing of a programme, where the audience for which it was intended look at or hear it via playback machinery. In the verbal sense, it splits up into two words; you play back a programme on playback equipment.

plot (*BT*) a plan, to show either where everything goes on the stage and set or where the lights are to go.

point of view (*VT, film, ST*) *see* **POV**

polecat (*VT, film, BT*) a metal tube jammed between two walls or between floor and ceiling. It can then be used as a support for several lights.

popping and banging (*sound*) undesirably high level of noise on the p and b sounds when someone is speaking into a **microphone**. A serious nuisance, especially if the person articulates well and the mike is not very sophisticated. Can be corrected by moving the mike a bit further away, and sometimes by asking the speaker or performer to slur his or her speech a bit.

portrait format (*ST*) an image or picture in the upright position – higher than it is wide. Arises when you turn a **35 mm** camera round through 90°. Very occasionally the need arises for a portrait-format **shot** in a **show**, in which case the original slide has to be cropped top and bottom and a special **mask** put round it. Portrait format is therefore not popular among slide-makers.
See also **landscape format**

post-dub (*sound*) *see* **overdub**

post-production (*VT, film*) the period between the end of taping or filming and the actual finished product. Mainly consists of **editing**, **dubbing** sound, finalising the **master** and either getting tape copies made or film prints.

post-sync (*film*) abbreviation for **post-synchronisation**.

post-synchronisation (*film*) sound, including dialogue, is re-recorded after the shooting has been done. Basically necessary when the original material was shot with undesirable **ambient noise** or with poor sound recording.
See also **dubbing**

POT (*VT, film, sound*) stands for a potential **out-take**. Any part of a production which is of dubious importance or quality.

potential out-take (*VT, film, sound*) *see* **POT**

P

POV (*ST*, *VT*, *film*) stands for point of view. A **script** term, e.g. 'Cut to new angle; from interviewee's POV.'

power (*BT*) electrical power. Sometimes a problem in **venues** located in exotic sunshine-havens (popular for conferences) when frequent thunderstorms and less than efficient utilities companies mean power failure is likely. When picking such venues, it's always prudent to book one that has its own electricity **generator**, or hire one in for the **show**.

practical (*VT*, *film*, *BT*) any **prop** that functions normally, rather than being a dummy or a model.
See also **unpractical**

pre-amp (*sound*) a secondary amplifier which goes as near as possible to the source of the electrical circuit – a **microphone**, for example. The idea is that the pre-amp improves the signal-to-noise ratio between itself and the main amplifier.

pre-fade listen (*sound*) a device in a recording studio which allows the **engineer** to check on a **fader** to see if it is being properly fed with input.

pre-production (*VT*, *film*) the period before you actually tape or film your **production**. This is the time when you write and finalise the **script** and **storyboard**, **cast** any actors, hire your **crew**, arrange any **locations** that are needed, plus all the ancillary items like crew accommodation, costumes, **props**, etc.
See also **post-production**

presentation (*BT*) a general term for any live speech, performance, etc. Can include **speaker support** slides, **modules**, even projected films and videotape. What's important to remember is that although parts of a presentation may be pre-recorded, the overall thing is one or two human beings presenting, live, to an audience of human beings – the machines act purely as back-up.

presentation unit (*ST*) any portable, reasonably self-contained device which plays back a slide–tape programme.
See also **Caramate, desk-top unit**

presenter (*VT, film, BT*) someone who presents a **programme**. This can mean that he or she is a combination of **anchor** and **narrator**. For the most part, presenters are seen as well as heard. They can also do their own **interviews**. Busy people.

preview (*all*) an occasion whereby a client can see or hear what his or her production is like before it is completely finished. *See also* **light-box preview, on-screen preview**

P

principal photography (*film*) the activity which takes place when a film is actually in **production** – when it is actually being **shot** – rather than at **pre-** or **post-production** stages.

print through (*VT, sound*) when magnetic tape is tightly layered round and round a spool and then stored for a while, some of the signal information can spread from layer to layer. This can give rise to problems when that tape is eventually **played back**, e.g. unexplained echo on a sound tape. This effect is called print through.

problem (*BT*) problems in business theatre **shows** can be anything from mild concern over a missing cable to a polite euphemism for an unmitigated disaster. However, business theatre problems, like World Wars, tend to bring out the best in people. **Crew** members are trained not to panic and can be reassuringly inventive if an alternative needs to be dreamed up.

processing (*ST, film*) the actual developing and printing of exposed film.

producer (*all*)
(1) in VT and film the producer is the chief organiser of a **production**, with little creative input – that's left to the **director** and **scriptwriter**.
(2) in slide–tape productions the producer also acts as the director and is usually the person who dreams up the whole **show**, although he or she will not necessarily write the **script**.
(3) in sound the producer will direct the recording **session**, as well as organise it, and will have a great deal of say in how the performers behave and how the **mix** is done.

(4) for business theatre *see* **conference producer**.

production (*all*) a general term, meaning a project, **programme**, film, recording, etc. With sound and business theatre, a project is in production when it is actually being made. The only areas in which the terminology is more specific are in VT and film; a project is in **pre-production** before photography takes place, in production when it is actually being taped or filmed, and in **post-production** when it is being **edited** and finished.

production assistant (*VT, film*) slight misnomer here because the production assistant nearly always assists the **director**, not the **producer**. He or she will take careful note of all the **takes**, their duration, whether they're good or not, etc. In a VT **studio**, he or she will actually speak the countdown and other instructions to the **floor manager**, cameramen, etc., on the director's command. This person will also assist the director during **post-production**.

production company (*all*) a company which works directly for a client and handles all the creative initiation – **scripts**, **storyboards**, etc. – plus the financing and administration of a project. Bigger production companies will also have their own facilities, so all or most of the production can be made in-house. Smaller production companies, of the one-man-and-dog variety, have to hire in everything from **scriptwriter** to cameraman. The advantage of this, though, is that the small company can pick the most suitable people from the selection of **freelance** talent available. Big production companies, although they do use freelancers as well, tend to use their own staff as much as they can, whether they're suitable or not.
See also **facilities house**

production crew (*BT*) strictly speaking, the **producer**, his or her assistant, the **script** editor, and anyone else who deals directly with the clients and their activities. This is to differentiate them from: the **stage crew**, who organise things **backstage**; the **rigging crew**, who set things up before the **show goes up**; and the **technical crew**, who run all the lights, **projectors**, sound, etc. Mind you, unless you're talking about a mammoth-sized show, you'll find that everybody belongs to the production crew and mucks in on every job that has to be done.

production manager (*VT*, *film*, *BT*) on larger **productions** a production manager will often be hired – generally freelance – to take some of the heat off the frantically over-worked **producer**. The production manager will be in charge of hiring, running and looking after the **technical** and/or **stage crew** and equipment, leaving the producer free to run the production side and pacify the client.

production schedule (*all*) a list of dates by which various stages of **production** should be complete. Usually prepared by the **producer** or the **production manager**.

product launch (*BT*) *see* **launch**

professionalise (*BT*) a polite term used when telling a client his or her own speech **script** is sub-standard. For a **scriptwriter** to professionalise a speech can mean anything from a gentle tidy up to a complete rewrite.

programme (*ST*, *VT*)
(1) as a noun, the correct term for a slide–tape or videotape production. Slide–tape programmes are also called **shows** but an original videotape production is always a programme – never a film. Videofilms are the taped copies of *Star Wars* that you hire from your local video rental shop to keep your kids amused on a wet Sunday afternoon.
(2) as a verb, the act of assembling all the slides for a show, loading them into **magazines**, feeding instructions into the machine or computer, plus recording **pulses** on the audiotape.

programmer (*ST*, *BT*) the person who **programmes** a **show**. Programming is a highly skilled job; good programmers earn a lot of money and deserve every penny of it. With large **projector rigs**, with anything up to sixty projectors to keep busy, you need to use a computer for programming; the programmer therefore must know how to be a computer programmer, as he or she will effectively be writing the software that drives the show. However the programmer also needs

143

considerable creative talent in order to use his or her technical
knowledge to create the most interesting and exciting effects.
Not an easy job, especially when you think that an average
three-hour business theatre presentation with, say, four
modules and six or seven speeches, will contain anything up to
5,000 **cues**, each cue or slide change requiring one complete
set of instructions keyed into the computer. Often a
programmer will also drive the projection rig at a business
theatre event.

projector (*ST, BT, film, VT*)
(1) modern slide projectors are a far cry from the old magic
lanterns. These days they're small neat boxes with a powerful
light and lens. The rotary **magazine** of slides sits elegantly on
top and the whole assembly can be fitted into a shopping bag.
(2) film projectors are bigger, especially when you get into **16
mm** and **35 mm**.
(3) videotape projectors are becoming more popular. Some
come in whole units with their own screen, but in business
theatre the current favourite can either **front project** or **back
project** on to the normal screen used for slides. The on-screen
quality is not as good as film or 35 mm slides, though.

promo (*all*) abbreviation for promotion, as in sales promotion.
Many of the **productions** in this business are used for sales
promotion purposes – short videotaped programmes to be
shown in stores, slide–tape programmes that are shown repeat-
edly on exhibition stands, audio recordings of a shop's best
buys of the day being just three examples.

props (*ST, VT, film, BT*) abbreviation for properties. Any
loose object, other than clothing or jewellery, which is used to
accessorise a **set**. A prop can be anything from a nail file to a
10-ton truck.
See also **practical, unpractical**

proscenium arch (*BT*) in a traditional-style theatre the
proscenium arch lies above the stage, parallel with the edge
nearest the audience, separating the upper part of the
performing area from the auditorium.

pull back (*VT*, *film*) a camera direction. It means to pull the whole camera and mounting assembly, on its **dolly**, backwards while **shooting**. This gives the impression that the image is gradually disappearing towards the horizon.

pull focus (*VT*, *film*) to pull focus is to change the focus of the camera from foreground to background as the subject or performer moves. Taping or filming doesn't stop while this is being done so it requires the steady hand of a trained **focus puller**.

pulse (*ST*) the electronic signals on the audiotape of a slide–tape presentation. These pulses drive the projectors.
See also **pulsing**

pulsing (*ST*) the act of putting electronic **pulses**, or instructions, on to a spare **track** of the audio tape that goes with a slide–tape **programme**. When the tape is played back, the pulses will tell the **projectors** – electronically – what to do at given times. The pulses are put on the tape by a skilled **programmer**.

punch up (*all*) to increase or activate something, from the colour or brightness of a videotape image to the **levels** in a sound recording **session** or **mix**.

pup (*VT*, *film*) a small variety of **key light**. Smaller still is the baby pup or **baby kicker**.

Q

Q & A (*VT*, *sound*, *BT*) stands for questions and answers. A structured interview with questions and answers so arranged that the interviewee, who is likely to be an expert of some kind, can get over a message. A more interesting way of putting information over than merely sticking the expert in front of the camera to talk in a monologue.

Q lock (*VT*, *sound*) a device which locks audio recording equipment, electronically, to the **time code** of a videotape recording. This means that during sound recording, editing, mixing, etc. the sound tape will be automatically synchronised to the videotape picture. Although sound recording studios which have a Q lock facility normally make a fairly hefty charge for its use, it is well worth the money; it saves a lot of time.

QTV (*VT*, *film*, *BT*) a brand name for a type of **teleprompter**, similar in operation to **Autocue** systems.

quadrophonic (*sound*) sound which has been recorded through four or more input tracks, and is played back split among four output channels. This is especially useful with music, or complicated soundtracks, played back in a large area; the effect it gives is very impressive. There is also 'false' quadrophonic playback, which consists basically of two stereo output systems run together.

Quantel (*VT*) a brand name for a range of machines which generate **digital effects**. Sometimes used as a general term for these effects, albeit wrongly.

R

rack (*film*) to adjust the film in a **projector** so the edges of the film don't show up on screen. When this does happen, the film is **out of rack**.

radio microphone (*BT, VT, film*) a **microphone** with no wires – or not so as you'd notice, anyway. Hand-held versions have a built-in radio transmitter, signals from which are picked up at the main sound **desk** and put through the **speakers** in the normal way. Radio **lapel microphones** will have a wire running down through the speaker's clothing to a small transmitter which is worn strapped to the belt or round the back. This transmitter's signals are also picked up and put through the main sound system. Radio mikes are used in videotape or film work where the **presenter** has to move around a lot, demonstrate machinery, etc.; they remove the danger of the presenter tripping over a wire. In the old days, radio mikes used to run on similar frequencies to those of fire stations and cab companies, which provided considerable amusement for crews, particularly if, halfway through a financial speech, you heard 'Cab to number 67 Acacia Avenue, roger' coming through all 900 watts of sound system. However today's radio mikes have been greatly refined as a result.

rag (*BT*) any stage curtain which is pulled back horizontally in two halves, rather than flown upwards.

raster (*VT*) a picture which is unmodulated and consists merely of the horizontal lines.

ratio (*VT, film, ST BT*) the width of any screen compared to its height.

rationalisation (*film, VT*) the adaptation of films shot for the

147

silver screen to fit into the different shape of a VT **monitor**. Involves careful thought and skilled **telecine** work.

recce (*ST, VT, film, BT*) abbreviation for reconnoitre or reconnaissance; pinched from army usage. The recce is the fact-finding trip you make to a **location** or **venue**, prior to **production**, to see whether it is suitable for what you want. In business theatre you'll also be looking for suitable places to build **sets**, hang lights, plug your machinery in and so on.

recording to picture (*sound*) putting a **narration** on to a video-tape or film production is best done with the **voice-over** artiste keeping one eye on the visual side of the actual production. He or she will sit in a soundproof area, equipped with a screen or VT **monitor**, and record the narration while viewing the film or tape.

redhead (*VT, film*) a light, made from fibreglass, which has a variable beam and power of around 800 watts.

red noise (*sound*) any sound which gives a greater variance in the low frequencies.

reel (*film, sound, VT*)
(1) a reel of film is any film wound around the metal cart-wheels used for projecting. In feature films, a reel is of a standard length of either 2,000 or 3,000 feet. In feature films you'll sometimes hear the length of a movie measured in reels instead of hours and minutes. You also refer to reels of video and audio tape. Also, sometimes, called a **spool**.
(2) although strictly speaking a reel is a film term, in this case it spills over into VT as well. Most **production companies** and many **freelance directors**, **producers**, etc., compile excerpts from their best work into a reel, in order to show prospective clients a brief example of what they can do (also called a showreel). Advertising creative people will also have a reel of their best commercials, to show when job-hunting.

reel-to-reel (*sound, VT*) loose tape which goes from reel to reel, as opposed to **cassette** or **cartridge** tapes, which are locked into their little boxes and can't be edited or tampered with.

spin (*ST*) a technique, usually involving **graphics**, whereby an image revolves on screen. Requires several **projectors** to do it properly without the image appearing to turn jerkily.

spin-timed (*sound*) this is a very rough method of checking the time or playback length of a tape recording. You do it by running the tape through a machine on fast forward and either check its length in seconds or on the footage counter. Obviously this is only an approximation of the true time, and can lead to embarrassing silences if used as the sole method of timing. However, it's useful for preliminary **editing** purposes.

spiral (*ST*) a technique, usually involving **graphics**, whereby an image either spins out of nothing out to a large picture on screen, or the other way round. Requires several **projectors** to do it properly so the spiral doesn't look jerky.

spit sock (*sound*) the foam 'sock' which is sometimes put over a microphone. The idea is to deaden any little **ambient noises**, plus the hisses and pops some people emit when they speak.

splice (*film, sound*) to splice film or tape is to join two separate lengths together when **editing**. A splice, as a noun, is a join in film or audio tape.

split focus (*VT, film*) between the devil and the deep blue sea! When you're **shooting** two objects, one in the foreground and one in the background, if you focus on one the other will look very hazy. Split focus solves the problem; you focus bang in the middle, thereby giving both objects a similar look.

split screen (*ST, VT, film*) split screen is when you show two or more separate images on the screen area at any one time. These images may be identical, to create a special effect, or different.

spool (*or* **reel**) (*sound, film*) the round device around which audio tape, videotape or film is wound.

spotlight (*VT, film, ST, BT*) any light which points in one direction only. Most spotlights are movable, so you can alter the direction in which they point. There are many different types of spotlight, and they are classified in this book under their individual names.

sprocket (*ST*, *film*) comes from the movies. Sprockets are teeth on a little wheel in the camera or **projector**, correctly spaced, which fit into similarly-spaced holes along the side of the film. The idea is to hold the film in place as it's going through the **gate**. With **slides**, though the film doesn't touch the gate, you still refer to sprockets. In this case they're the little knobs inside the mounts used for the **35 mm** transparency film. The holes along the side of the film are predictably called sprocket holes.

spud (*VT*, *film*) a pole which fits into a **turtle**, so allowing the final connection to a light. The end result of a light attached to a spud fitted into a turtle is a light on a three-legged stand.

sputnik (*VT*, *film*) a 2-kilowatt focusing light.

squawkbox (*VT*) a two-way communication system that connects the **studio** floor with the main control **box** in a television or videotape studio. Users on the studio floor will receive and send their messages over their **headsets**; those in the control box will hear messages over a small loudspeaker and send their messages down a **microphone** mounted on the control panel.

squeeze (*sound*) to squeeze a recorded voice **track** or other sound means to take off much of the treble and bass noise, leaving the kind of sound you get when you listen to someone talking to you over the telephone. In fact a recorded voice treated this way is sometimes called a **telephone voice**.

Squeezoom (*VT*) a trade name for a machine which electronically generates **special effects**, normally enlarging or shrinking an image on screen.

stage (*BT*)
(1) (noun) the performing area of a business theatre **set**.
(2) (verb) to organise and put on an event on stage.

star filter

stage crew (*BT*) the crew members who actually operate any equipment to do with the presentation on **stage**, as opposed to equipment operation which takes place elsewhere in the theatre or room.

See also **production crew, rigging crew, technical crew**

stage directions (*BT*) can be confusing as they are the precise opposite of some camera directions, e.g. stage left would be camera right, and so on. Here are the basics: stage left – the right-hand side of the stage, looking at it from the audience; stage right – the left-hand side of the stage, looking at it from the audience; upstage – the part of the stage at the back, furthest away from the audience; downstage – the part of the stage near the **footlights**, nearest the audience.

stage left/right (*BT*) *see* **stage directions**

stage manager (*BT*) the person who manages all the organisation and administration of what goes on stage. He or she will ensure that **props** are in good condition and in their right places, that all equipment is working and ready on time, and that all the **stage crew** are doing their jobs properly.

stagger through (*BT*) a very rough kind of **rehearsal**, not necessarily in show **running order**, to give all speakers a chance to familiarise themselves with the **set**, the **venue**, their speeches, the **teleprompter** if there is one, and their visual material.

stand by (*all*) an expression meaning to be ready and poised to go into action. A **director** will tell a crew to stand by when he's about to start **shooting**; a business theatre **producer** will tell various equipment operators to stand by a few seconds before the **go** command.

stand-up (*BT*) any comedian or compère who does his or her turn by merely standing up and chatting into a **microphone** in front of the audience. This sort of artiste doesn't normally need any **props** other than, perhaps, a few small bits and pieces he or she carries.

star filter (*ST, film, VT*) a camera **filter**. This variety creates

167

radiations shaped like our rather clichéd image of a star, emanating from highlights in the picture. The effect is attractive when used sparingly.

Steenbeck (*film*) a brand name of a popular make of film viewing and **editing** machine.

stereo (*sound*) when the sound is played back split into two, with complementary **tracks** of sound coming from two **speakers** or sets of speakers. Sound can also be recorded in stereo, which means that one sound or group of sounds is recorded on one track, and the remainder on the second track. Sound which is recorded on more than two tracks can be distilled down to stereo – this is very common practice, particularly with music.

sting (*sound, BT*) a musical sting is a very short little musical phrase, almost like a brief fanfare. This is used in many instances, almost as punctuation to a production. You may also hear of an AV sting used in business theatre; this is a short, mini-**module** lasting up to ten seconds or so, with a few slides and a bit of music and used to act as a link between one speaker and the next.

stobing (*VT*) a visually disturbing effect created when the **raster**, or horizontal, lines in the video picture clash with the patterns or colours of either scenery or performers' clothing.

stock (*all*) any raw, unexposed or unrecorded film or tape. This is a word you'll see in budget breakdowns; the cost of some stock, especially large-format videotape, can represent quite a significant sum in the final reckonings. Normally production companies do not throw in the cost of stock, i.e. raw materials, with the cost of actually making a film, programme or recording; it's charged separately.

stock shot (*VT, film, ST*) another way of saying **library film** or library shot. It means a **shot** or **sequence** – and in the case of slide–tape it can mean one still photograph – which has been produced by others and can be hired in for inclusion in your production. The cost of hiring it in is likely to be far less, in time and money, than sending people out to get an original version.

stop (*or* **f stop**) (*ST, film*) a diaphragm of a stills or film camera lens controls the amount of light that's allowed to get through. The degrees by which the amount of light varies are called stops or f stops.

stop motion (*film*) a technique whereby you can make static inanimate models and other objects appear to move on film. The object of stop motion is to stop the film every few **frames**, or even run it one frame at a time. Each time the camera stops, you move your models a little bit, so the end result on film looks as if they're moving by themselves. A very popular technique within children's television.

storyboard (*BT, ST, VT, film*) a storyboard gives clients and producers an idea, on paper, of what the eventual production will look like. Usually a storyboard is done on normal sheets of paper, with a row of little boxes – to represent **frames** or **sequences** – down one side. In the boxes an artist will draw an approximation of what would be appearing on screen at that particular point. On the opposite side of the paper you'll often see the relevant words from the proposed script to match the picture.
See also **film storyboard**

strike (*BT*) not a mass walk-out of crew. To strike a **set** means to dismantle it after a **show**.

strobing (*VT, film*) a lighting term. It happens when the frequency of light variation is exactly synchronised with action of some kind. Most experts say you shouldn't have lights flashing at any higher rate than twenty times per second, otherwise th effect can wreak havoc with your eyes.

studio (*all*) the places where various forms of work are created, e.g. recording studio, film studio, photographic studio, etc. Studios tend to be where the nuts and bolts of creative initiation take place – as against administration which is done in offices, videotape **editing** which is done in an **editing suite**, or film

169

processing which is done in a laboratory. The studio is the 'factory floor' of the business.

subtitles (*ST*, *film*, *VT*) **captions** superimposed over the main picture, which give the gist of the action on screen. In this business, subtitles are used mainly when producing foreign-language versions of programmes or films, to give a translation.

sun gun (*VT*, *film*) a small battery-operated portable light.

super 8 mm (*film*) 8 mm film with sound recording facility. Like its cousin, **8 mm**, it's popular with amateurs; it's also popular with small groups, clubs and so on to show educational or special interest films. Provided your projection **throw** and screen size are small, the quality's not too bad, and an 8 mm **projector** is a lot handier to carry around and set up than its **16 mm** big brother.
     See also **70 mm**, **35 mm**

superimposition (*ST*, *film*) to place one image over another and photograph both together. If this applies to two full-**frame** images you'll get a dreamy, surrealistic effect – provided it's done well, otherwise you'll just get a mess. Another kind of superimposition is to put a **caption** of some kind over another image, preferably with enough solid colour space somewhere to accommodate the caption.

super slide (*ST*) a larger format of **slide**, where the image area is larger than that of **35 mm**. However it fits into the same size of slide **mount**.

surround sound (*BT*) an effect which, using special **speakers** and a **panpot** device, makes the sound seem to circle or move totally around the audience. Used for **special effects** in more elaborate business theatre events.

swifter (*BT*) a taut steel wire along which objects or people can slide or 'fly' across a **stage**. Comes from conventional theatre use.

sync (*VT*, *film*, *sound*) abbreviation for synchronisation. To say that something is in sync means that its timing perfectly matches that of another component of the production, e.g. if sound is in sync on film it means that the separately recorded **soundtrack** has been matched up to the action on the film.

See also **lip sync, post-sync**

synopsis (*ST, VT, film*) *see* **outline**

synthesiser (*sound*) a musical instrument, usually based on a keyboard principle, which can electronically copy the sounds of other instruments, e.g. violins, trumpets and so on. Synthesisers can also be **tweaked** up to create a variety of unusual **sound effects**.

S

T

tag (*or* **tag line**) (*all*) the tag is the last line of dialogue spoken in a production. You're most likely to hear the word in the context of a radio or television commercial, or any other short sales-orientated production. The tag, or tag-line, is the last thought left with the viewer or listener, so it's quite important that it should be snappy and memorable.

tail out (*film, sound*) when a copy of a film or audio tape has not been re-wound after its previous use, and the beginning of the production is at the wrong end, it is said to be tail out.

take (*VT, film, sound*) one continuous unbroken bit of **shooting** or sound recording. If a take is less than satisfactory, it will be done again and again until all concerned are happy about it. Takes are normally numbered by the production staff and the most acceptable one is noted for later **editing** purposes.

talk back (*sound*) a system which allows **crew** members to talk to one another from one place to another via a fixed built-in **microphone** and **speaker** system. Usually the microphone is situated in the control room and anyone sitting in there can flick the switch to talk to someone sitting in the sound-proofed **studio** area. The person on the receiving end hears the talkback track over the **cans** or through a small **monitor speaker**, and can reply just by talking into the regular microphone.

talking head (*VT, film*) any person who appears in a production, usually shot from the waist or shoulders up, talking straight **to camera**. A typical example of this is the well-known style of the television newsreader. Talking heads are very popular in corporate and training programmes and films, but too much use of this approach, without **cutaway** visuals to break it up, tends to be boring and tedious.

172

Tannoy (*sound*, *BT*) trade name of a brand of loudspeakers used for public address and business theatre presentations, in sound studios, etc.

tape (*all*)
(1) (noun) can refer to either sound tape or videotape, depending on the context.
(2) (verb) it usually means to videotape a shot or programme; it is sometimes used instead of the word record in the sound capacity, but more usual jargon phrases for that are to put down or **lay it down**.

tape–slide (*or* **slide–tape**) (*ST*) some people say tape–slide instead of slide–tape; to my knowledge there is no right or wrong way around. The choice is up to the individual!

TEAC (*ST*, *sound*) trade name, and an acronym at that, for a particular brand of four-track portable tape recorder/playback unit, very popular for use within slide–tape and business theatre circles.

technical crew (*BT*) a term sometimes used in large business theatre events to differentiate between the people who move things around and work the machinery near the **stage** area (**stage crew**) and the people who operate the **projectors**, the computer that drives the stills projectors, the lighting **rig**, the sound rig, **teleprompt** machine, etc. Also differentiates them from the **production crew**, that consists of the **producer**, assistant producer, script editor, etc., and the **rigging crew** – the people who set up all the equipment before the event.

technical rehearsal (*VT*, *film*, *BT*) a **rehearsal** done largely for the benefit of the crew and any other technical people in a **production**. Any involvement on the part of performers or speakers is essentially to enable lighting, sound **levels** and so on to be checked against them. At a business theatre **venue** the technical rehearsal is normally done before any of the other rehearsals take place.
. *See also* **dress rehearsal, stagger through, top and tail rehearsal**

telecine (*VT, film*) a machine – or a process – which generates television pictures, and/or videotapes them, from film.

teleconference (*BT*) a comparatively new and interesting way of bringing **speakers** together from all over the world for a conference. This is achieved over a private television broadcast, via **DBS** if necessary. Each group of people is shot live on camera and the images are then transmitted to **monitor** screens in the presence of all groups involved. The principle works much as does a networked live television broadcast. Naturally, it is expensive, but if the alternative is for a company to pay out a small fortune in hundreds of first-class return air fares from the four corners of the globe, plus executive-style accommodation in one central **venue**, teleconferencing can suddenly begin to look more viable.

telephone voice (*sound*) a recorded voice **track** where the voice sounds as though it has come through on a telephone call. It is achieved by recording the voice normally in a **studio** and then altering the sound electronically during the **mix** afterwards. It's a popular effect for light or comical soundtracks, radio commercials, etc.

See also **squeeze**

teleprompter (*VT film BT*) known, in the trade, as the idiot box. Here's how it works. (1) The **script** – to be spoken by a **presenter** or a **speaker** at a conference – is typed on a continuous roll of paper. This is sometimes nicknamed the loo roll. (2) The roll is put through a machine which moves the script through a **gate**. (3) A **closed circuit TV** camera is pointed at the gate and its contents and transmits what it sees to a small **monitor**. (4) Now, here's where we hit the fork in the road. At a conference, or any live performance, the monitor will be placed at the bottom of the speaker's **lectern**. The lectern will have a conveniently transparent glass top through which the image of the script is passed, ending up on either one or two glass screens. These are placed perpendicularly to the ground, in front of the speaker's nose. From the audience's side they look like clear glass but, because of a special reflective coating on the glass, the speaker can see his or her words perfectly, and can read them out while appearing to speak naturally from memory. With a film or videotape camera, however, you have that same piece of reflective glass right in front of the lens. The camera, like the conference audience, sees straight through the glass but the presenter reads away merrily. The speed at which the loo roll goes through the gate is, of course, controllable. At a conference, where the speaker has plenty on his or her mind, there is normally a trained operator who controls the speed while listening to the speaker's voice through a **headset**. There is even scope for the speaker to stop reading for a bit and **ad lib**; not a disaster, provided he or she goes back on script, taking up exactly where the written part was left off. However, speakers who do not return to the same bit of the script cause many an incident of high blood pressure among teleprompt operators – as they also do to entire conference crews. In the case of videotape or film presentations to camera, the method varies. Sometimes a trained operator works the speed control of the teleprompter in much the same way as in conference work; in other circumstances the presenter can control the speed by pressing a foot or knee lever.

telescope (*VT*) a device that uses a series of retractable tubes to suspend studio lights at different heights.

teletext (*VT*) strictly speaking this is a broadcast television term and therefore does not belong in this book. However, teletext is used for business purposes so it may just qualify! Teletext is the one-way information service offered by the broadcast TV channels. In the UK there are two at the time of writing; the BBC's Ceefax and ITV's Oracle. Home viewers, with the appropriate adjustments made to their own television sets, can call up a large selection of 'pages' of information, from stock market prices to cricket scores. Teletext systems are in use in many boardrooms and management offices, too.
See also **videotex**

theme (*BT*) the overall concept of an entire conference or event. The theme, which is normally something all-encompassing and general, will be carried through all the visual material, the tone of the speeches, pre-recorded **soundtracks** and even to the **set** design, accompanying leaflets, etc. In one large event the theme was 'take off' with the company concerned. As the theme suggested air travel, the whole set and auditorium area were designed and constructed as the interior of an airliner, with the stage created to look like a giant cockpit. All announcements were made in the style of those in an airport, and suitably dressed 'stewardesses' ushered delegates in and out of the room. The opening and closing **modules** of the presentation included very loud and realistic sound effects of a jumbo jet taking off and landing, plus **multi-image** sequences on the main screen simulating the pilot's view of take-off and landing. Expensive, but highly effective.

35 mm (*film, ST*)
(1) in film (movies) terms, this is the width of film used for features and big entertainment productions – what you see in your local cinema. Its width requires big, heavy and expensive equipment, both to **shoot** and project it. The high standard of quality it offers is necessary when you have to project over a long **throw** in a cinema on to a big screen. However, it represents a bit of overkill for non-feature work.
(2) the main width of stills film used in **slide–tape** photography.
　　See also **8 mm, 70 mm, 16 mm, slide, super 8 mm**

thread (*film, sound, VT*) to thread a film **projector**, an audiotape or VT recorder or **playback** machine is to put the end of the film or tape concerned through all the necessary slots and passages so that it is ready to be activated by the machine.

throat (*VT, film*) the gap left in one wall of a **set** to permit access to a camera.

throw (*VT, film, ST, BT*) the distance between **projector** or projectors and the screen on which they must 'throw' their images.

tilt (*VT, film*) a camera direction. As the word suggests, this manoeuvre means that you tilt the camera up or down on its mounting.

time code (*VT*) a recorded electronic signal in a videotape programme. This gives a unique number to each span or 'frame'

on the tape – each 1/25th of a second – to allow easy synchronisation.
See also **sync**

tit (*all*) slightly sexist term for any form of button that must be pushed in order to operate a control.

TK (*VT, film*) stands for **telecine**.

to camera (*VT, film*) someone who speaks – with or without the aid of a **teleprompt** device – while looking directly at the camera lens is talking to camera. Why the definite article is left out of the phrase, I can't discover; such is the jargon of the business!

tone track (*sound*) a recording of random background noise to provide the right atmosphere for a **production**.

top and tail (*all*)
(1) a method of **rehearsal** in business theatre, normally used when a conference or presentation has already taken place once and has then gone on tour with a **roadshow**. Once all the speakers and performers have rehearsed the show properly and done one full performance, there is no further need to rehearse everything in subsequent **venues**. However chances are each venue will be substantially different in shape and size to the previous one, so every time the **set** is rigged anew, speakers and performers need to get acquainted with their new surroundings; this is done by using the top and tail technique. Basically, each speaker and performer gets up on stage and does the very beginning of his or her presentation, skips the bulk of it in the middle, and goes straight on to the wind-up and ending. **Modules** are started, skipped through and ended. In this way the logistics of a show, predominantly the handovers from speaker to speaker and the links, along with all the technical functions like lighting **cues**, sound cues, module cues etc., are practised without having to go through the entire content.
See also **dress rehearsal, stagger through, technical rehearsal**
(2) any treatment of a soundtrack or programme where the main bulk of its content is topped and tailed with another style. For example, a videotape programme can consist mainly of

interviews, with a studio **anchor** presenter doing an introduction and a conclusion. In that case the studio anchor sections are the top and tail. A soundtrack that consists mainly of music can be topped and tailed with a **voice-over**, etc.

top shot (*VT*, *film*, *ST*) a camera **shot** taken overhead, either directly above or almost above the subject concerned.

track (*sound*, *VT*, *film*)
(1) abbreviation for **soundtrack**.
(2) slang for a piece of music, e.g. "Love Me Do' was the Beatles' first track to make the charts.'
(3) used in sound recording to identify a channel of sound input or output, e.g. four-track sound **studio**, twenty-four-track studio, meaning the studios have four and twenty-four available sound recording channels.
See also **multi-track**
(4) a camera direction, involving the camera moving towards (tracking in) or away (tracking out) from the subject along a specially-built track. The end result is similar in effect to that of a **zoom** but is more subtle.
See also **tracking shot**

tracking shot (*VT*, *film*) any **shot** in which the camera moves backwards or forwards, following the action – usually one person talking **to camera** while walking along, or two actors in supposed conversation while strolling down the street, etc. These shots can be done with the camera hand-held or with the camera pushed or pulled on a wheeled **dolly**. However in large-budget productions special tracks will be laid down along which the camera mounting can travel smoothly and evenly. Improvisation is possible with tracking shots, too; on one training film about orthopaedic patients the cameraman sat in a wheelchair while his assistant pulled him backwards and the subject followed along being filmed while walking.
See also **track**

training film (*VT*, *film*) a film or videotape **programme** that serves an educational purpose. Sometimes you'll hear them referred to as 'video films' (which is not only incorrect but impossible!). Videotape tends to be the preferred viewing medium these days; video cassette **playback** machinery is normally idiot-proof, whereas threading up a film **projector**, setting up the screen, etc., involves more time and energy. However, the original material may be shot on either film or tape. Training films will either be specially commissioned and made to measure for a company, or will be made 'on spec' about general topics, and sold or hired out to interested parties.

trannie (*ST*) nickname for, and an abbreviation of the word, transparency. In theory it can refer to a transparency of any size, but is usually taken to mean the **35 mm** transparency used in most **slide–tape** programmes.
  See also **slide**

transfer (*ST, film, VT, sound*) to transfer a programme means to re-record it either from one medium to another, e.g. slide–tape to videotape, or from one format to another within the same medium, e.g. sound from **1-inch** eight-track tape down to audio **cassette**.

transparency (*ST*) *see* **trannie**

traveller (*VT, film, BT*) a curtain that runs along a sliding track.

tray (*ST*) a plastic rectangular device with rows of racks to contain **slides**. Mounted slides can be placed in sequence on a tray and then put over a **lightbox** so production people and clients can view them in order. Needless to say, trays have sufficient slots and open areas along the rows to allow light through the slides. Trays also offer a tidy way of storing slides in their correct order, often stacking up in specially-fitted cupboards in the production area of a **production company**'s premises.

treads (*VT, film, BT*) any steps or stairs built into a **set**, whether they're to be used for **crew** access or as a part of the **props** for the taped, filmed or on-stage **action**.

treatment (*ST, VT, film, BT*) a fairly detailed, written explanation of how a **production** will look and sound. The treatment

179

is the intermediate stage between the **outline**, which gives a
brief overview of the concept, and the **script**, which spells it all
out in full. The treatment is sometimes dispensed with,
especially when the programme duration is short; in this case,
it is just as easy and more satisfactory to proceed straight from
outline to script.

trim (*VT*, *film*) to change the carbon rods in an **arc** light. The
word comes from the traditional trimming of the wick of a
candle.

tripod (*ST*, *VT*, *film*) a three-legged stand on which pieces of
equipment can be mounted for extra stability. Tripods can be
used for stills cameras, videotape or film cameras, lights, sound
speakers, etc.

tromboning (*VT*, *film*) the excessive use of a **zoom** lens on a
camera, creating the effect of too much backwards and
forwards movement on screen.

trough (*BT*) a long metal container which holds stage lights.

turtle (*VT*, *film*) a three-legged floor stand into which a light,
connected by a **spud**, can be fitted.

TV safe (*ST*, *VT*) if a slide–tape programme is later to be
transferred to videotape, as is very common these days, the
main picture area of each **slide** must conform to the **aspect ratio**
of the television screen, which is slightly different to that of
projected slides. **Artwork** and photography must be done
bearing this in mind; it is made TV safe. (Also video safe.)

tweak (*all*) to fine tune and improve the performance of any
piece of equipment.

tweaker (*VT*, *film*, *BT*) a small screwdriver used by electricians
and carpenters.

twinkle (*ST*) a very fast **snap change** effect using two **projectors**, alternating from one to the other and back again. On
screen the image either appears to be 'twinkling' or else can

appear to move rapidly, e.g. a person running on the spot, waving a hand, etc.

2 inch (*VT*) videotape which is 2 inches wide. This is what is known as full **broadcast standard** of tape and provides excellent quality. It is also very expensive as it and its surrounding equipment are larger and more complex than that which is involved with, say, **low band** or **high band**.

2¼ square (*ST*) a 2¼-inch (54 mm) square slide. Larger than the standard **35 mm** slide, not many projectors can do justice to them.
See also **slide**

two-four-six (*VT, film*) small wooden blocks, glued like a small set of stairs, each about 2 inches high. These are used by the **grips** in a **production** to lay and strengthen the camera tracks for **tracking shots**.

two-shot (*VT, film*) any **shot** in which there are two human figures.
See also **one shot**

typesetting (*ST*) part of the **artwork** process of making **slides**. When words and/or numbers are required for a slide, the artwork will be drawn up in the **studio**. Some of the lettering and numbers may be done using instant dry lettering there and then, but for larger amounts of words and numbers a specialist typesetting organisation will be brought in. They use machinery that produces the necessary letters and figures either mechanically or photo-electronically, and prints them out on to shiny white paper. The paper is then cut into strips and the strips pasted down on the artwork, with the words and numbers in their correct places.

U

Uher (*sound*) a brand of **reel-to-reel** audio tape recorder, using ¼-inch tape. This brand of machine, along with a few others, was very popular some years ago for **location** radio news reporting. The quality is excellent, but today's vastly improved audio **cassette** recorders provide almost the same quality with far less weight to hump about over the reporters' shoulders. Uher's and their equivalents are still used for more elaborate location work, reel-to-reel tape being more easily edited.

ulcer (*VT, film*) a light diffuser made of a board from which various portions have been cut out. This is then placed in front of the light.

U-matic (*VT*) a videotape format created by the Sony organisation of Japan. In the UK there are two qualities of U-matic, **low band** and **high band**. U-matic comes in a **cassette** format.

umbrella (*VT, film, ST*) a deflector placed behind a light. It is normally shaped like, and is operated in the same way as, a real umbrella.

uncut (*film, sound*) a film or audiotape is uncut if it has not yet been edited.

undercrank (*film*) to run a camera more slowly than the normal speed of 24 frames per second. If the resulting film is projected at normal speed, the screen effect will be very fast motion, in the style of the old silent comedy films. You can also use normally-shot film and undercrank the projector, which gives the opposite effect – **slow motion**.
  See also **overcrank**

unpractical (*VT*, *film*, *BT*) a dummy or model **prop**.
See also **practical**

updating (*ST*) **slide programmes** can be easily updated by replacing existing slides with new ones. Provided the new slide fits in with the existing **soundtrack**, the process is simple; there is no need to reprogramme or change anything else. It is for this reason that slide–tape shows are often preferred to videotape or film, which are both considerably more difficult and expensive to update.

up-front (*all*) the way in which all **productions** should be billed to the client! The fact that a **production company** is required to lay out often quite large sums of money to **facilities houses** and other suppliers means that clients are normally expected to pay to the production company a substantial percentage of the total budget at **pre-production** stage. With small productions, and in particular small sound recording projects, it isn't always necessary, but clients are expected to settle their bills with production companies promptly.

upstage (*BT*) *see* **stage directions**

V

valentine (*VT*, *film*) a soft light of either 1 or 2 kilowatts power.

VCR (*VT*) acronym for videocassette recording, or videocassette recorder. The first is the **software**, the second is the recording/playback machine.
See also **cassette**

venue (*BT*) the place where a business theatre event takes place. This is more usually a theatre or conference suite of an hotel, exhibition centre, etc., but it can just as easily be a stately home, a zoo or even a marquee in the middle of a field.

VHS (*VT*) acronym for video home system, developed by the JVC organisation of Japan. This is one of the two small **cassette** formats suitable for use in the home and for small-audience business, corporate or educational playback. The other small format is **Betamax**.

video disk (*VT*) the same idea as a sound disk, but producing a picture as well. At the time of writing, video disk can only be used for **playback** – you can't record directly on to it. Also at the time of writing there are two main types of video disk in existence: a mechanically-produced variety which spins twenty-five times faster than an LP record; and the optical laser-light-produced variety which spins fifty times faster than an LP record. Video disk playback equipment costs roughly the same as a good quality videotape **cassette** playback machine, but of course you can't use the video disk equipment for recording off **broadcast** television or anything else. The advantage of video disk playback over videotape is that the quality of image tends to be sharper, and disks take far longer to wear out than do tapes. Thus in an educational context, say,

184

where programmes will be viewed dozens or even hundreds of times over, video disk may be preferable. Programmes to be transferred to video disk can be originated on videotape or film, although some experts say that a better result is obtained using **16 mm** film as the origination medium.

Video 8 (*VT*) a home video format, now offered by several different manufacturers. Although it is sometimes confused with **8 mm film**, there is no connection apart from the fact that in this instance the videotape inside the cassette is eight millimetres wide. The cassettes used are about the same size as the audio compact cassette. Video 8 cameras, sometimes known as Camcorders – depending on the manufacturer – contain video recorders built in. This means that when you want to play back your videotape, you simply connect the camera unit to your television set; there is no need for a separate video playback machine. Video 8 machines, or Camcorders, are great fun for home use but, for now at least, don't offer a great deal to the professional or institutional programme maker, as the quality is not good enough.

video film (*VT*, *film*) a physical impossibility if you think about it. You can either have a videotape programme, or a film. All other terms are technically wrong, although some are less unacceptable than others, particularly in the case of the word video, which only means vision but which can be used to describe anything from a **VHS cassette** to a rock music promotion on **broadcast** television. The only time when the use of 'video film' is almost logical is in the context of a feature film available for home viewing on videotape. These are the video films you rent from a local shop or club – major movies which have done the round of cinemas first and have then been transferred to videotape for domestic sale or hire.

video playback (*VT*) playing back a videotape programme, or a section of it. This can be done using equipment in the video **editing suite**, although the term actually means playback on anything, even home videocassette recorder.

video projector (*VT*, *BT*) a few manufacturers have, at the time of writing, produced machines which will project videotape programmes on to either a separate or incorporated screen. The quality of this projection, although much improved since the early models, is still far (in my opinion) behind that of **16 mm** film and **35 mm** slide.

video recorder (*VT*) a loose term which covers any machine that records videotape, other than the camera itself. In other words, it can mean a video**cassette** recorder, or any other machine in an **editing suite** which performs that function.

videotex (*or* **viewdata**) (*VT*) videotex is an information service available to people with a suitably wired-up telephone connected to a video **monitor**. In the UK British Telecom's branded service is called Prestel. The main advantage of videotex or viewdata over teletext (at the time of writing) is that videotex can be inter-active, i.e. two-way. Teletext, for the moment at least, is still one-way only as it is **broadcast** rather than sent down the telephone line.

video transfer (*ST, film, VT*) the act of transferring slide–tape or film to videotape. Slide–tape programmes are transferred using a **multiplexer**; film is transferred using a **telecine** machine.

video wall (*VT, BT*) is a device whereby a number of video monitors are stacked up to form a giant multi-screen viewing wall. Videotape programmes or **sequences** can be made to show one normal-sized image repeated on each of the screens, or one large image – with the relevant portion on each screen – covering the entire 'wall'. Because you benefit from the brightness and sharpness of each individual normal-sized monitor, video walls create a much sharper, brighter effect than you would get with videotape conventionally projected from a single source on the same screen area.

viewdata (*VT*) *see* **videotex**

viewfinder (*VT, film, ST*) the part of a camera – video, film or stills – that you look through with one eye. Even though you're not necessarily looking right through the lens itself, the viewfinder, if it is accurate, will show the precise frame area as it will come out on the videotape or film that you shoot.

vignette (*VT*, *film*, *ST*) a **mask** placed in front of the camera lens. It is so cut and shaped that it allows only a portion of the view to be shot, for example creating a keyhole effect.

vision mixing (*VT*) blending together a variety of images into one videotape or, more usually, into one television programme. The vision mixer is the person who will blend from one camera to the next in a live multicam television production, following the commands given by the **director**.

visualisation (*ST*, *BT*) the work done by the **visualiser**. Sometimes, in a small **production company** and/or on a small **production**, it is the **producer** or even the **scriptwriter** who performs this function. With many slide–tape programmes and **modules**, and certainly with most live speeches, the **script** is written first and then visualised afterwards. This is where you can see one of the most obvious differences between slide–tape and motion picture programmes as, with the latter, words and pictures are nearly always created simultaneously.

visualiser (*ST*, *BT*) as in the advertising context, a visualiser is someone who interprets the written ideas of the **scriptwriter** and **producer** in terms of drawn images. He or she may also add quite a lot of ideas, to flesh out and develop the visual side of a **programme**, **module** or **speaker-support** presentation. The visualiser will then draw up a **storyboard** which, once approved by the client, will form the basis of the show's visual content.

VLS (*VT*, *film*, *ST*) stands for very long shot.
See also **shot lengths**

vocals (*sound*) a music business term meaning all the singing parts in a piece of music, be they **backing** or lead vocals (performed by the principal singers or stars).

Vocoder (*sound*) a machine which creates special effects, using the basis of a human voice **track**. This is one of the machines which can produce 'robot' or 'Martian' voices. You feed in a recording of someone's normal speaking voice, then play along with the voice track on a piano-like keyboard. This creates the sounds of chords, but expressed as the words of the voice track.

An interesting effect, but not one which should be over-used – too much becomes confusing to the listener.

voice over (*ST, VT, film, sound*) a voice which is heard but not seen. This invisible person speaks a **narration** to picture in the case of slide and videotape programmes and films. With sound, these people are still called voice overs, although of course any voice on a **soundtrack** with no picture will technically be 'over'. The term voice over, or VO, is informally used to describe both the person and the job, but technically it should only be used for the job. The person is usually an actor or a newsreader, and likes to be called a voice artiste. VOs are normally hired from specialist agencies, although many **producers** have a direct line to a few actors and broadcasters who do a little moonlighting. In the UK, voice artistes are paid fees as agreed with the actors' trade union, Equity. These vary according to the job, starting fairly low for radio commercials, working up through slide–tape programmes to non-broadcast videotapes and films, to fairly hefty sums for television commercials.

vox pop (*all*) from the Latin *vox populi*, voice of the people. Vox pops are **interviews** conducted at random with people in the street in order to elicit their views on whatever topic the interviewer may throw at them. They form a useful short interlude in many types of production, whether to underline research results, make a marketing point, or even just to raise a few laughs and lighten an otherwise heavy subject. They can be produced on VT or film, or even just on a **soundtrack** for slide–tape or audio-only playback.

VTR (*VT*) stands **for Video Tape Recording, or sometimes Video Tape Recorder.**

V 2000 (*VT*) one of the very early videocassette formats, developed by Philips and Grundig. The earliest tapes were of one hour's duration only, and were very bulky compared to today's **VHS** and Betamax **cassettes**. Later, these tapes came in several lengths, up to four hours. The playback machinery is not often seen now, and I think it can be safely assumed that the format is no longer one of the major types.

walk a flat (*BT*) to carry a **flat** in an upright position. To walk a flat up or down is to raise or lower it by hand.

walk in/out (*BT*) the function, and the period of time during which it takes place, of the audience walking in and sitting down in the **venue** auditorium – or, getting up and walking out. It's used as a compound noun, e.g. 'We start walk-in at 9.15 sharp.'

walk-in music (*BT*) music used as background sound during **walk-in** and, for that matter, during **walk-out** as well. Walk-in music tends to be of the easy-listening variety, rather like that which you hear in North American lifts, and in luxury department stores.

wallet (*ST*) a clear or translucent plastic pocket into which a number of **slides** can be inserted for storage. Some wallets come equipped with a metal rod across the top, hooked at each end, so that the whole assembly can be stored in a standard office filing cabinet.

wallpaper (*VT, film, sound*) any pictures or sound which act as 'fillers' or general background material. With most **location** work it is a good idea to shoot or record some general views, **establishing shots** and general noise – voices, machinery, etc. – over and above what is stated on the **production schedule** or shot list. This is to act as standby material should any extra requirement come up unexpectedly; such material is known as wallpaper.

warm up (*VT, film, sound*) to warm up an interviewee. In **interviews** it is rarely advisable, though sometimes necessary, to begin taping or filming straight away without first talking

189

informally to the interviewee to set him or her at ease. This preamble is known as the warm-up; it's commonly practised by the broadcast TV and radio organisations and helps to ensure a more relaxed, more fruitful interview.

Wessmount (*ST*) a popular brand of slide **mount**, suitable for most slide–tape programmes and **multi-image modules**.

wet hire (*all*) an expression used to show that equipment hired comes with all necessary personnel to operate it. Opposite of **dry hire**.

whip pan (*VT, film*) the rotation of a camera in a complete 360° circle. This technique is often used to suggest the movement of the **action** or story to another **location**, where the next scene is happening 'simultaneously'.

white noise (*or* **acoustic perfume**) (*sound*) an overlay of background or **wallpaper** sound intended to have no specific character of its own but to drown out a selection of irritating unwanted sounds that would otherwise prove distracting.

wild (*VT, film, sound*) this term is used most in sound recording studios, although in theory it can apply to *VT* and film as well. To record something wild is to record it out of sequence. It is then edited into its proper place later. For example, if a **narration** (**voice over**) **track** is recorded in its entirety, and afterwards someone wishes to re-do one line or two, these will probably be recorded 'wild' after the main **script**, and edited in afterwards. This takes up rather less time than if the voice artiste were to re-record the whole script.

window effect (*ST*) a type of pseudo 3D effect, which is cheaper than genuine 3D. Audiences must still wear polarised glasses, although this is not the real thing.

wind-up (*all*) final few lines of a spoken **script**; the final summing up or motivational thought before the end of a **production** or presentation.

wings (*BT*) the area immediately to either side of the **stage**, normally screened off by **flats**, the latter sometimes placed at a slight angle.

wipe (*VT, film*) an optical (film) or electronic (videotape) device used for quick changes from one picture to the next. A line appears at one edge or corner of the screen and moves across it, obliterating the old picture and pulling the new one in with it. This line can either be hard and sharp, or soft-edged; it can move horizontally, vertically or diagonally.

word slide (*ST, BT*) a **slide** which has only words and/or numbers on it – no pictures, graphs or charts.

wow (*VT, film*) slow variations of speed that affect the quality of recording on both video- and audiotapes.

wrap (*VT, film, BT*) a word that signifies the end of a day's work, be it a VT or film **shoot**, a business theatre rehearsal or performance, e.g. 'It's a wrap – see you all tomorrow!'

write-on (*or* **Ektographic**) (*ST*) a clear, plain **slide** upon which you can write whatever you want (Ektographic is Kodak's trade name for such slides). Write-ons, suitably annotated to indicate what is to come, can be used as substitutes for final slides in programming, when some of the finished products are not yet ready. The programme can then be **previewed**, albeit with gaps filled only by handwritten notes on the write-ons rather than a full complement of finished slides. When the final slides are completed, the write-ons are pulled out of the **magazines** and replaced by the finished ones, put in as **drop-ins**.

Y

yashmak (*VT, film*) a type of diffuser that covers only the lower half of a light. The term is derived from the mask that covers all but the eyes of a devout Muslim woman.

Z

zip pan (*VT*, *film*) a very fast **pan** by the camera, of anything up to 360°.

zoom (*VT*, *film*) a camera direction. To activate a **zoom lens** to either close in on the subject or to pull away from it.

zoom lens (*ST*, *VT*, *film*) any type of lens, whether for still or motion picture, that has a length of focus which is variable – in the case of motion pictures, variable even when shooting is going on.

Z

BIBLIOGRAPHY

Cheshire, David (1982) *The Video Manual*, Mitchell Beazley,
London.
Foss, Hannan and Elliott, Geoff (loose-leaf) (1980) *Video Production
Techniques*, Kluwer, Brentford.
Green, Jonathon (1984) *Newspeak*, Routledge & Kegan Paul,
London.
Moorfoot, Rex (1982) *Television in the Eighties: The Total Equation*,
BBC, London.